NORTHAM, WESTWARD HO! & DISTRICT

THROUGH TIME

Julia & Anthony Barnes
& Maureen Richards

AMBERLEY PUBLISHING

Acknowledgements

Special thanks to David Gale for his permission to make use of his research on Northam. Also to the Westward Ho! History Society. We would also like to thank Peter Keene, for the use of material from his book *Westward Ho! Against the Sea*, published by Thematic Trails. Our thanks also to Stan Andrews, Helen Beer, Bideford Archive, Bideford Library, Carol Brown, Burton Art Gallery, Wendy Clarke, Dinny Cope, Cross House Cottages, Durrant Hotel, Mary Elliott, Tim Gale, Hallsannery Wedding Venue, Frank Heard, Morans Restaurant, Anne Nielson , Lt-Col Michael Portman, Mrs R. Prouse, Royal North Devon Golf Club, Sir Hugh Stucley, Douglas Whitehead, Yeolden Hotel.

First published 2013

Amberley Publishing
The Hill, Stroud, Gloucestershire, GL5 4EP
www.amberley-books.com

Copyright © Julia & Anthony Barnes
& Maureen Richards, 2013

The right of Julia & Anthony Barnes & Maureen Richards
to be identified as the Authors of this work has been
asserted in accordance with the Copyrights, Designs and
Patents Act 1988.

ISBN 978 1 4456 1882 1 (print)
ISBN 978 1 4456 1861 6 (ebook)

British Library Cataloguing in Publication Data.
A catalogue record for this book is available from the
British Library.

Typesetting by Amberley Publishing.
Printed in Great Britain.

Introduction

Northam and Westward Ho! – two such different villages, despite both having originally been part of Northam. It's easy to forget how large Northam once was – possibly once the 'North Hams', as there are South Hams in South Devon. It once included Appledore, Westward Ho!, the Orchard Hill and Raleigh Hill areas, and even Bideford right up to Northdown House (the old convent school); indeed, it continues again on the far (Torrington) side of Bideford, known as Northam Without or Northam Ridge.

Its history can be authentically traced back 6,000 years, with the discovery of a submerged forest and kitchen midden in the peaty mound on Westward Ho! beach, left behind by Mesolithic hunter-gatherers, which is still exposed on the beach at low tide. At that time, these people inhabited a forest of oak, willow and birch in boggy ground and the remains of trees are exposed there still with their food debris – shells, hazel nuts, bones of deer and aurochs and wild boar – along with many flint tools, artefacts and scrapers. Back then, the sea was several miles away out in the bay, and at a much lower level relative to the land. In the 1980s, wooden stakes were found, probably dating from Neolithic times, which are thought to be the remains of fish traps and weirs.

Westward Ho!'s famous pebble ridge, still so much a feature of the area, has been retreating inland now for a very long time, and ever since the village's inception this has proved a troublesome and often devastating problem; inundating and wrecking buildings constructed too close to the encroaching sea, shattering the long hoped for pier, and even completely flooding the Burrows.

Named after Charles Kingsley's novel, Westward Ho! was planned carefully to be an elegant, spacious, beautiful private estate by the sea to rival Torquay and to be approached like any other grand private estate via two lodges and two private drives. It was laid out with supreme optimism and forward planning in elegant style, with new tree-lined roads, gracious hotels, baths, private schools, mansions, swimming pools, a health sanatorium, a pier and a promenade. Also built were a golf course, a railway, croquet lawns, social clubs, serviced beach bathing with bathing machines and attendants, and whatever else a monied leisure class might desire.

Sadly, the new resort, begun with such high hopes, never did even begin to rival Torquay. The railway never succeeded in being joined to the main line at Bideford, and because of this, and all its attendant problems, never paid its way. The sea destroyed some buildings and sapped confidence; the pier was destroyed by the fierce waves of the Atlantic Ocean; the two new schools lasted only a short time before closing; many of the villas and mansions remained unsold. With the decline of the servant classes, many of these mansions were too grand and spacious for more modern living and were divided into apartments, their gardens sold off for building development.

The Northam peninsula with its extensive coastline naturally developed as a seafaring and self-contained farming community. For hundreds of years it was very isolated from the town of Bideford by the difficulty of road transport crossing the marshy ground that lay between them, until Northam Causeway was built at last in 1439. Until this time, water transport was more convenient and the banks of the River Torridge and the Cleave area were the centre of Northam's industry, where hundreds of ships were built, lime burned and bricks made. Never a large village, Domesday records only twenty-eight villagers, eight slaves, a pigman, a fishery and two salt houses. With road improvements, it became popular with retired Army personnel and wealthy merchants, who built numerous beautiful mansions on its outskirts, many of which are still there today.

Northam Burrows, an area of some 260 hectares of sandy dunes and marshland, already gave common grazing rights in Norman times even though it belonged to the Lord of the Manor. Protected only by the pebble ridge, it has been flooded many times, but remains a valuable and much-loved asset to the area. It is host to the oldest golf course in England, which attracts golfers from all over the world to play its undulating and challenging links.

Westward Ho!

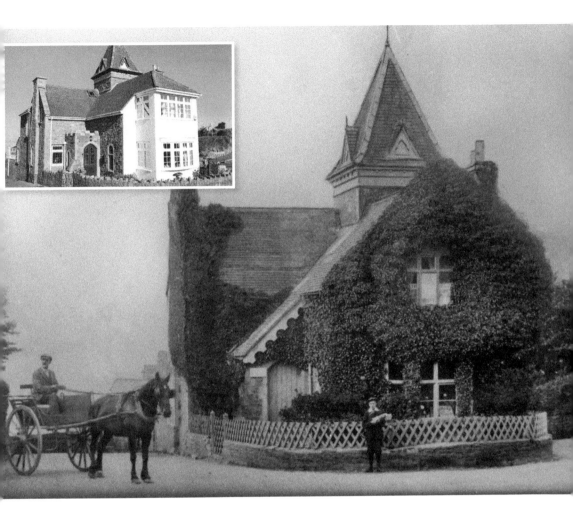

Upper Lodge, Bay View Road, Built 1866

Here is the picturesque original entrance to the new village of Westward Ho! It was all planned to resemble a grand estate, with a new drive constructed (on the left of the lodge) and this lodge house with gates across. It led straight down to the front door of the new Royal Hotel. The sign on the right reads, 'Jo presents dance bands', and the sign in the window advertises cycles for hire. Carriages waited here for the gates to be opened by the lodge keeper and for brake shoes to be fitted to the carriage wheels for the steep descent. Fosketh Hill, on the right of the picture, was the old road and Stanwell Hill (once St Ann's Well) the new road, but in 1870 an application was made to Northam Council for 'an order for stopping up Fosketh Hill for the New Road' so that from then on Fosketh Hill had gates at the top and visitors were obliged to use the new road. In the gardens of the lodge was a capacious reservoir together with a pumping house, which is still there, and supplied the new village of Westward Ho! This was filled with water pumped up from wells at Pimpley.

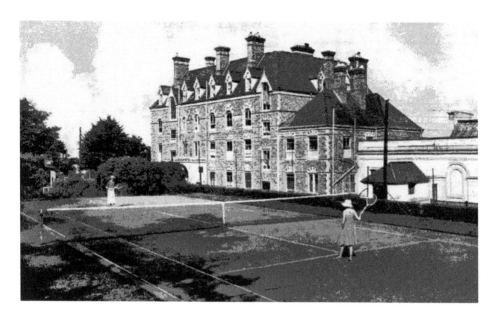

Royal Hotel and Tennis Court, Opened 1865

This rather grand Victorian Gothic hotel was originally called the Westward Ho! Hotel. At its opening, it was commented that 'it is not too much to expect that a second Torquay will arise in North Devon'. The hotel was a posting house, had thirty-three bedrooms, coffee rooms, reading, billiard and smoking rooms, and a swimming bath across the lawns with concert rooms. The company built a big annex called The Villa, now flats called Golden Bay Court 'for servants belonging to aristocratic visitors', with a station just below it. The entrance gate is still there, though twelve houses have been built on the site. Sadly, as Westward Ho! developed into a self-service resort, this grand hotel slipped out of favour. In 1963 it closed down, turned into flats, and ninety chalets were built in the gardens and grounds. Finally, it was demolished in 2000 and replaced by apartments called Ocean Park. Opposite the hotel and across the road were these grass tennis courts, seen here being used by two of the hotel guests in their long skirts. The entrance is still there, though twelve houses have now been built on the site.

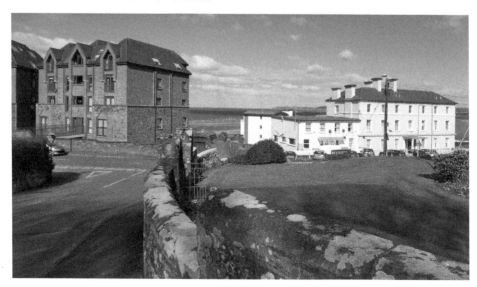

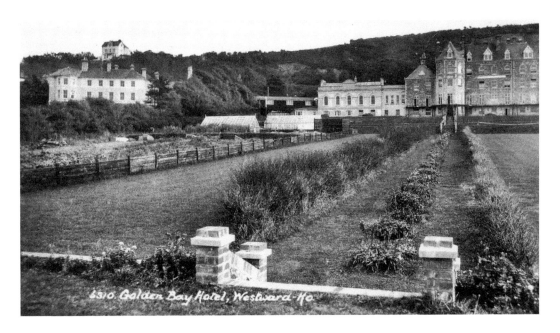

6310. Golden Bay Hotel, Westward-Ho

Royal Hotel Gardens

Seen above, the 75 acres of gardens and grounds were quite magnificent. At the back of the hotel were gardens, several grass tennis courts (one shown on the right), bowling greens and four croquet lawns. Grassy rides and hydrangea walks led down to the seafront and to the ladies' bath house. Horses for riding and posting were kept in the stables. Then there were hotel kitchen gardens and hothouses (shown on left of picture) where they grew their own food. Below, an artist's impression of Royal or Golden Bay Hotel. Before the days of the laws of misrepresentation, this delightful artist's impression of the hotel was circulated, showing the hotel grounds leading down by way of manicured flowery lawns onto a sandy beach where the blue sea laps gently.

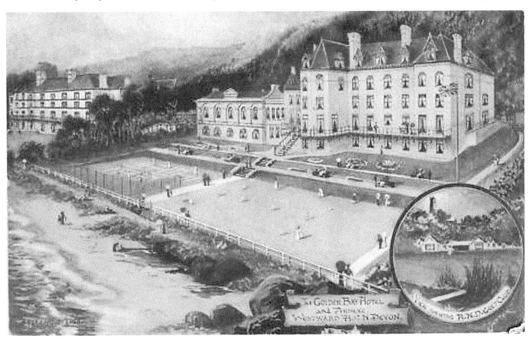

The Golden Bay Hotel
and Annexe,
Westward Ho! N. Devon.

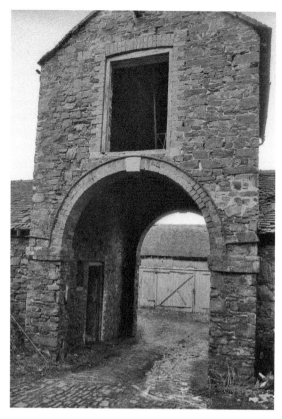

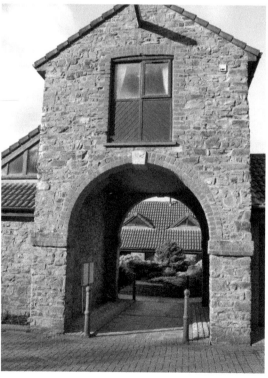

Royal Hotel Stables, Now the Rocks
When the Royal Hotel was built, these
old stables were already there across
the road, and they were converted and
extended for use by the hotel's guests,
their horses and carriages, and for a
public bar or 'tap' for the refreshment of
grooms, ostlers, coachmen and servants.
The hotel also served as a posting
house and the stables here housed the
horses for this service as well. The
hotel advertised 'Motors, Carriages and
Saddle Horses supplied on orders left at
the Office. Dogs per day 2/- if in private
rooms 1/- Large dogs can be kept in the
stables. Bicycles can be kept in garage:
3d per day, cleaning extra.'

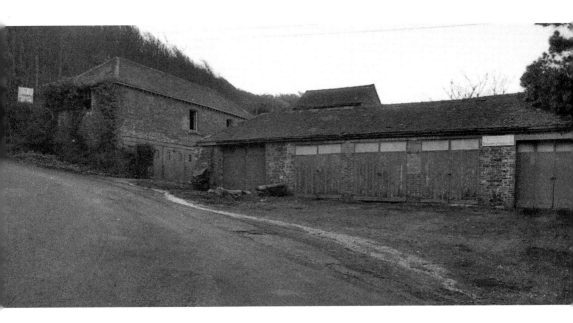

Royal Hotel Stables

Later, when transport had moved on apace, the hotel advertised a well-equipped lock-up motor garage for thirty cars instead. The old stables are still there at the foot of Stanwell Hill. For many years they lay derelict after the hotel ceased to be run as a hotel, but were eventually sympathetically and well converted into several attractive cottages, and the little courtyards and this archway preserved unspoilt. The hoist arm for raising hay bales to the hayloft is still in place.

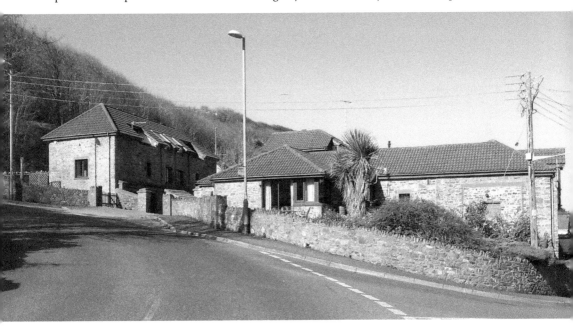

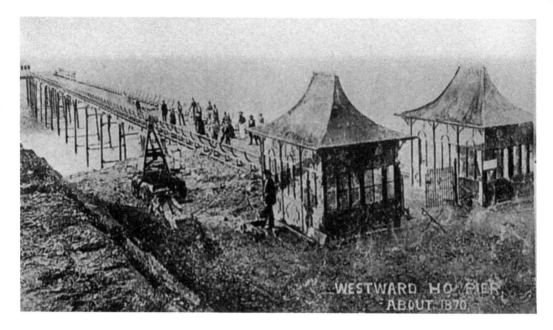

Westward Ho! Pier

A cast-iron pier 600 feet long and 16 feet wide was planned with timber decking. At the end a splendid bandstand and refreshment room were to be built, and work began in 1870. Some of the hard rock had to be blasted away. Disaster struck in October 1871 when gales snapped the cast-iron supporting pillars 'just like clay tobacco pipes'. The damaged pier was hastily repaired, and in 1873 it was opened at last, with 2*d* being collected from visitors as they passed the two attractive little toll houses at the entrance. More storm damage occurred in February 1880, and the whole project was abandoned as a failure; the pier was closed and demolished. Remains of the piles that supported the pier can still be seen at low tide by the side of Seafield House, and part of the decorative railings is at North Devon Maritime Museum at Appledore.

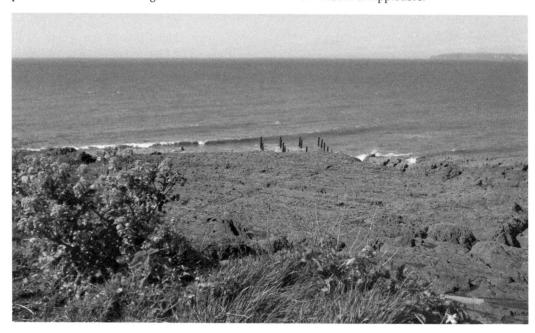

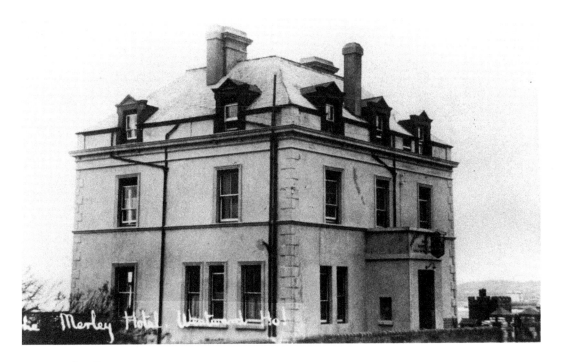

Merley House

Merley House was built in 1885 by George Molesworth, and it became the holiday home of the 9th Duchess of Manchester in 1918. It later became the Merley Hotel, as shown here. It was requisitioned in the war to house part of Highgate School when the school was evacuated from London. It was renamed the Headland Hotel in 1946. Braddicks bought it in 1951 and renamed it the Elizabethan in 1959. Now renamed again, it is the Pier House, a popular restaurant, with some of the finest views of Bideford Bay in North Devon.

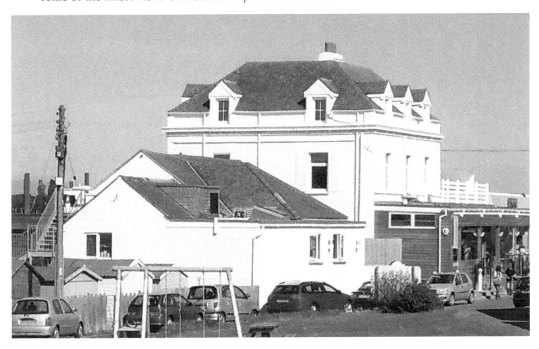

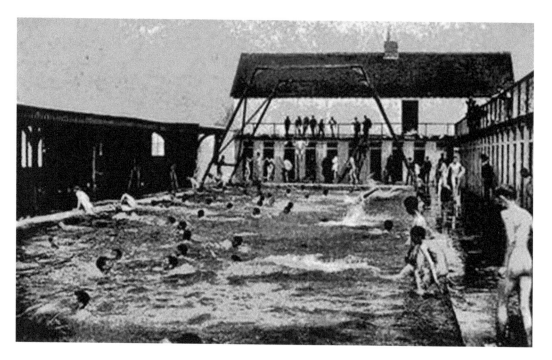

Nassau Baths/Patio Pool

The upper picture shows boys from United Services College using their school swimming pool, and it is obvious that the new school didn't rush to issue swimming costumes for them. Tourists were encouraged to use the baths in the school holidays, and in the 1950s and 1960s the venue became a very popular swimming pool and suntrap, changing its name to Patio Pool. The later picture shows the same view after closure when some attempts were made to transform it into a sunken garden, but it became derelict.

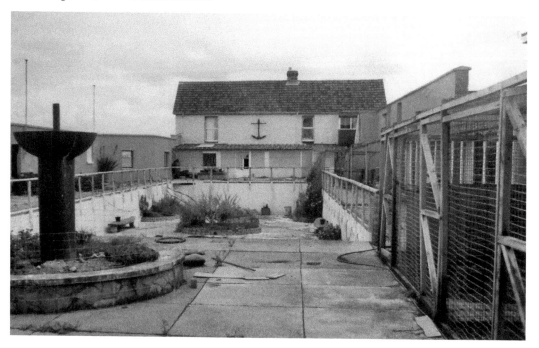

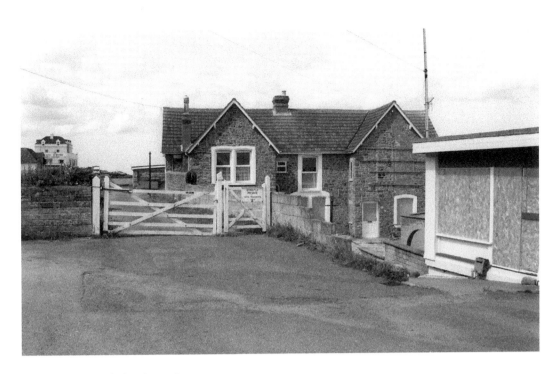

Nassau Baths/Patio Pool

George Molesworth opened United Services College in 1874 and soon decided that a swimming pool would give the school a distinct advantage. The baths were blasted out of the rocks and were opened in 1875, Nassau being a Molesworth family name. The pool was 8 feet deep and 130 feet long, and was filled with water from the sea by a powerful steam engine that could pump 700 gallons a minute. The pool was tiled and in the winter it could be mostly drained and used as an ice rink. Molesworth was never short of yet another ingenious idea. The railway ran right by the baths where the five-barred gate is shown. Finally, it was demolished and a large block of flats built and called Nassau Court.

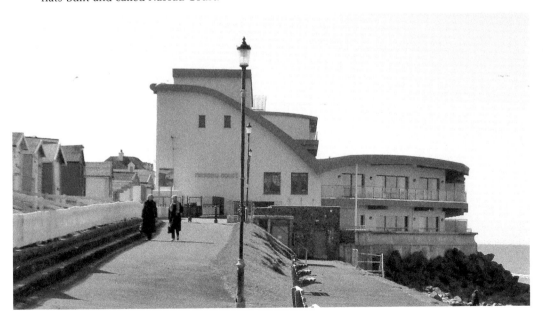

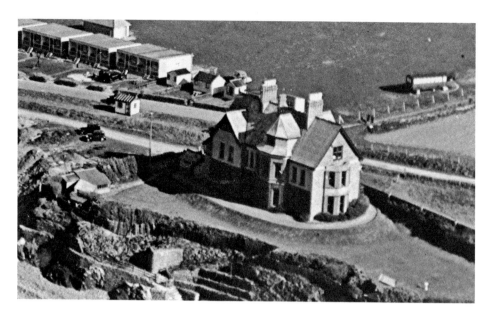

Seafield House from the North

Seafield was built in around 1885 by Brinsley de Courcey Nixon, a London banker, as a summer residence for holidays with his family. He actually died here when on holiday in 1903. The old photograph shows the private stone staircase down to the beach for family swimming and picnics. The rough Atlantic Ocean has not been kind to the sea edge of the gardens, though remains of the staircase can still be seen from the beach. Like so many other houses here, Seafield was requisitioned by the Army in the war and painted grey. In 1950 the house was sold at auction and advertised a conservatory entrance, dining room, butler's pantry, kitchen with Beeston boiler, scullery, servants' hall, extensive cellars, a maids' sitting room and ten bedrooms. Subsequently the house became a small hotel before falling into disrepair, becoming a rather well-loved romantic ruin of its former self as the sea continued to encroach on its beach-side location. Merley Road itself was constructed specifically to be an access road and drive to Seafield House, although the very old former road to the western end of Westward Ho! is still there as a bridleway at the foot of the Tors.

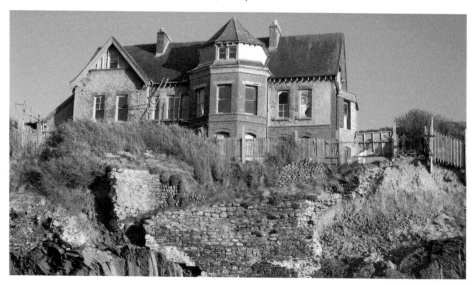

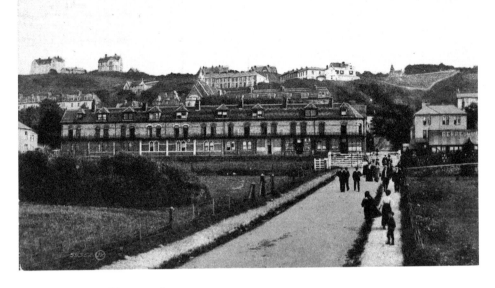

Station Road Looking South, *c.* 1910

This is a view up Station Road, now Golf Links Road, towards the level crossing by Westward Ho! station. The land on either side of the road is still undeveloped and just fields and hedges. The level crossing gates are closed and a train expected and the Station Café has 'Refreshments' emblazoned on the roof. During the war this café sold chips for 3*d*, but only if you brought your own newspaper to wrap them in! The station hall was known as the Drill Hall. There are no houses or shops yet on the seaward side of Nelson Road, and the house called Dormie behind the station is now the Fishing Shop, Summerlands. On the skyline from left to right are Edgehill, Drayton, then below is USC laundry house, High View Terrace, Fosketh House and Upper Lodge, with the triangular walls below it enclosing a reservoir.

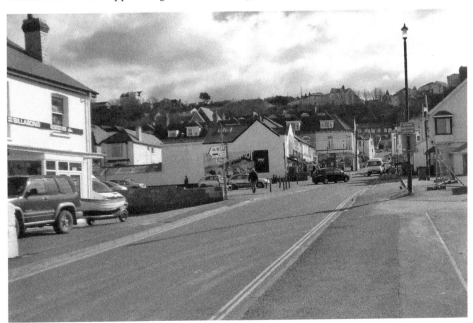

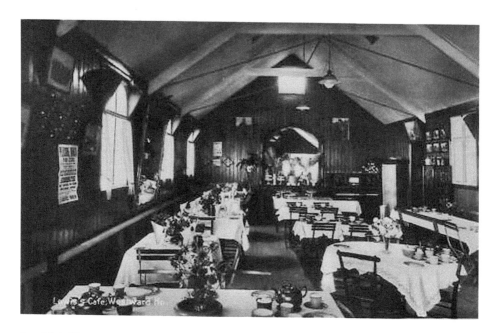

Lewis' Café

Built as a chapel for the village, this became Lewis' Café, and surprisingly it is still where it always was – in Station Road, now Golf Links Road, opposite the village green. Lewis also owned the Sunshine Café in Westbourne Terrace, and both were used by the military during the war to make camouflage netting. Sunshine Café then became classrooms for Highgate School when it was evacuated here. Later, Lewis' Café became an amusement arcade, but it has now gone full circle and become an upmarket restaurant again.

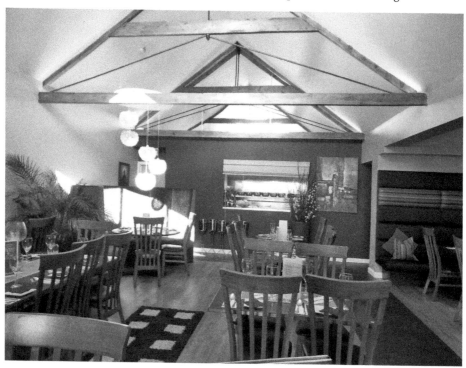

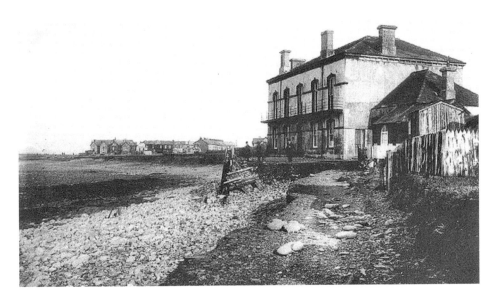

Old Bath House Hotel (Ladies' Bath)

Captain G. F. M. Molesworth built the Royal Hotel and the Bath House Hotel in 1866 and they were among the first buildings in the new Westward Ho! The Bath House was easily reached from the Royal Hotel as it was only a short walk across the croquet lawn. On the first floor, there was a large ballroom and also a balcony looking over the sea. Men could use the bath at certain prescribed times, though they mostly had to bathe in the sea or in one of the two rock pools excavated from the rocks, but had to change in the hired tents or bathing machines on the beach. The bath was filled with water pumped from the sea by steam engines. The train ran right by the hotel and there was a level crossing adjacent to it. Balls were regularly held in the ballroom: 'The balcony of the ballroom was decorated with foliage and gaily lit up with Chinese lanterns ... the ballroom was quite alive with flags and decorations and ... filled with merry dancers.' The dancing began at 10 p.m. and ended at 3 a.m. Later, the bath was filled in to make a garden for the hotel, which was used as a church on Sunday afternoons before the Anglican church was built. The whole complex was demolished and Horizon View apartments built in its place.

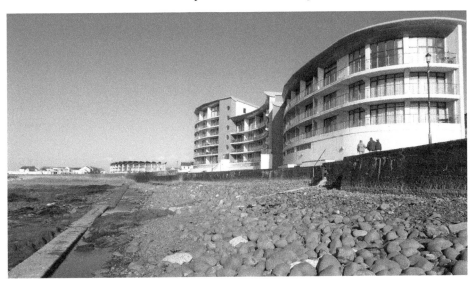

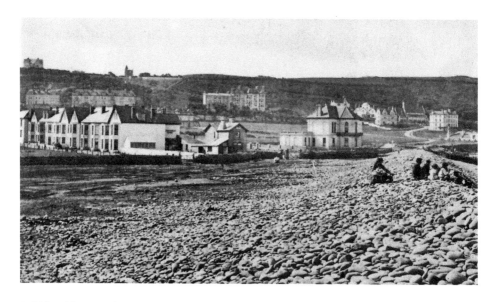

Pebble Ridge, 1876

A particularly interesting early photograph of the seafront and pebble ridge. The Union Club (middle), Lower Lodge to its left and the end of Westbourne Terrace have yet to be destroyed by the encroaching sea and the damaging pebbles being hurled against them. First, the cottages were plagued by sewage flowing back into the houses and contaminating the drinking water wells. There are no houses at all on the skyline of the Tors yet. Lower Lodge and the Union Club were built on what is now the beach in 1876 and moved to their present positions inland in 1879. This picture is taken from the same point as the previous one. It shows how far the ridge has encroached on the Burrows, and it is just possible to see the end of Westbourne Terrace, where six houses had to be demolished after wave damage in the late 1890s.

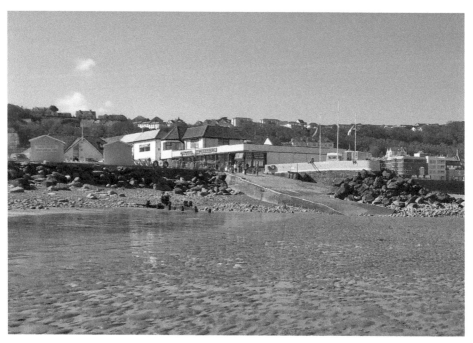

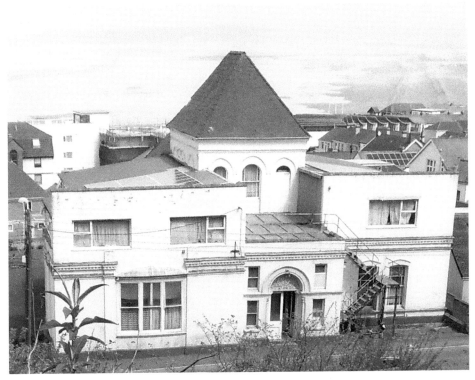

Union Club and Lower Lodge

Two lodges were built by the original Westward Ho! Development Company to guard the two principal entrances to their estate, and Lower Lodge, seen here on the left, guarded the eastern boundary. Both lodges had toll gates and people had to stop and pay to enter the new estate of Westward Ho! It was decided that Westward Ho! needed a new working men's club to be called Union Club, and it was built in its original position in 1876. Stormy seas soon began to damage it, hurling pebbles over the garden and grass in front of the club, and washed away the garden hedges. Water poured into the ground floor and damaged the furniture and there were fears that the clubhouse would soon be swept away. Lower Lodge was demolished hastily in 1879, only three years after being built, and rebuilt on Golf Links Road opposite the upper end of Westbourne Terrace – and it is still there. The Union Club also was quickly rebuilt further inland in Atlantic Way, and remained a club until it closed at last in 1958 and was converted to be Atlantic Flatlets. It is still there with the two crossed golf clubs over the front door and the original date of 1876 inscribed there.

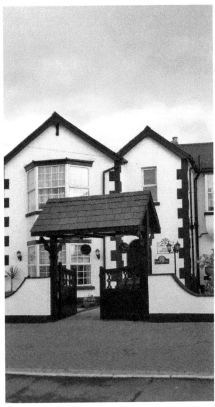

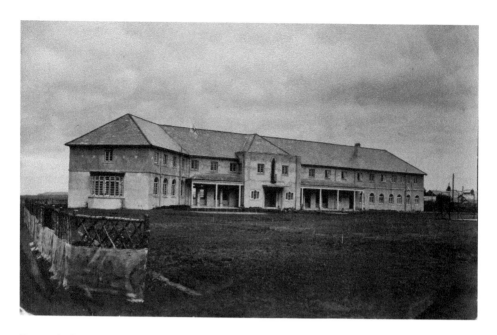

Dormy/Atlanta Hotel

Dormy Hotel opened for business in 1938, a neighbour of the North Devon Golf Club. It boasted that it was 'the most modern hotel on Devon's Atlantic Coastline standing in 10 acres of grounds by the beaches of Westward Ho! with a swimming pool, rock gardens, putting green, a private cinema, tennis courts, stables, golf on its doorstep and a ballroom, with fresh produce daily from own extensive kitchen gardens'. Later it was modernised with central heating and radios in every bedroom, and the name changed to Atlanta Hotel. Fire broke out on the night of 8 January 1970. The hotel was empty that night as it was closed for the winter, and the manager had gone out for the evening. Sixty firemen tackled the blaze, but it was all in vain, and the fire gutted the building. Some time later, the hotel was demolished and the grounds and field remain empty to this day with only grassy mounds as telltale signs that a hotel ever existed.

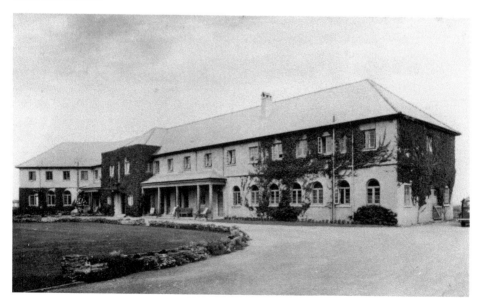

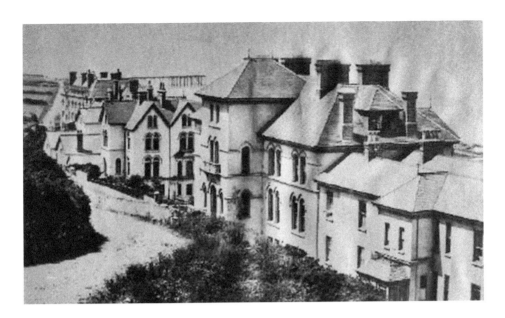

Fosketh Hill

The hill once came straight down at this point on an even more precipitous trajectory than now to the T-junction here. Its gradient was much too steep for any transport other than pack horses, so the line of the lane was altered, probably when Rowena and Torridge were built. At the time of the photograph, it is only a rough track with no retaining wall at the side. The new pier is clearly shown in the background. On the right is Rowena, built as an upmarket boarding house. The manager ran the livery stables nearby across the road where people could leave their horses (the 1880s version of our car parks) or hire transport to go out from Westward Ho! In the centre of the picture is Torridge House, another of Molesworth's attractive mansions, built as a private sanatorium but later converted to a hotel with twenty bedrooms. To the left of Torridge was its 'New Wing', added a bit later with additional bedrooms and a smoking room. This has now been demolished and only the foundations remain. Further down the hill is Golfstone, now a small hotel called Culloden, and then Manorville, which is now a youth hostel. The Royal Hotel is in the background.

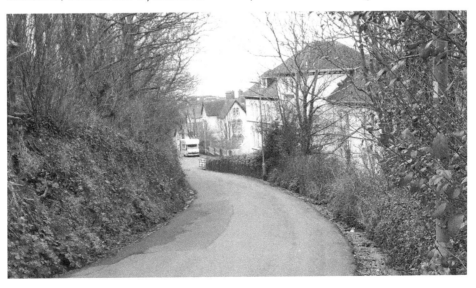

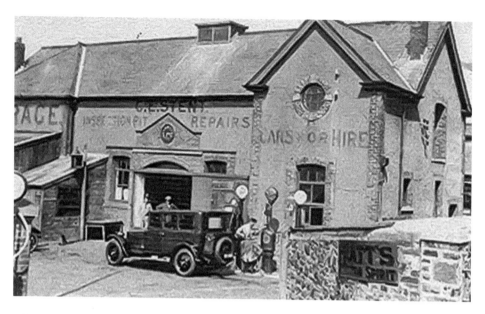

Old Golfstone Stables

At the lower edge of Link House grounds, these stables were built in 1901 with stable clock over the arched carriage entrance. Here there were two loose boxes, a coach house, two stables with stalls, a harness room and a loft over the whole of the ground floor for storing hay. In front were a large, walled yard and an enclosed field. In 1921, they were converted to a motor car garage and Mr Stent had new petrol pumps installed. Here advertising states 'Cars For Hire, Car Repairs, and Inspection Pit and Patts Motor Spirit'. The archway for carriages is still there, however, along with the old stable clock. In 1946, it became Nelson Garage, remaining so until 2006 when it was demolished and became Nelson Mews, a small, attractive close of town houses.

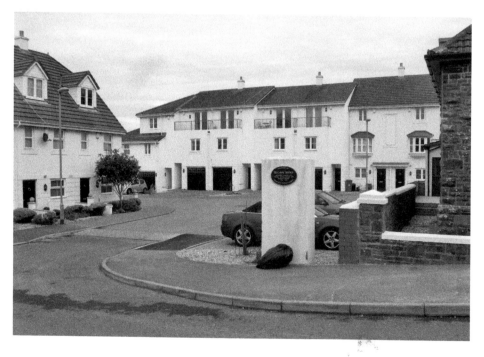

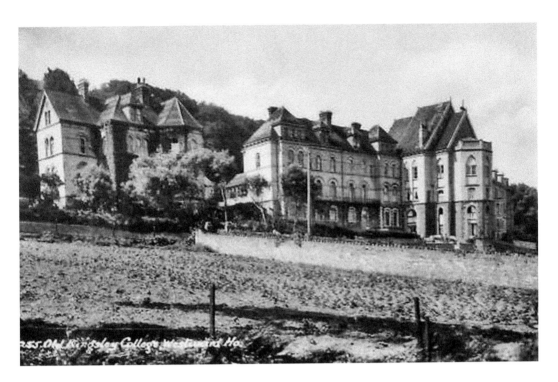

Kingsley College/Cleveland Terrace

Molesworth started a second college, but this time it was planned for the sons of doctors, lawyers and clergymen. He took over a terrace of seven houses in Cleveland Terrace. There was a ballroom and behind it the bakehouse and the laundry. Underneath the huge balcony were the stables and the coach house. The school only survived for four years, never paid its way and closed abruptly and mysteriously in 1885. The buildings were vacated in such a hurry that desks were left in the classrooms and the beds in the dormitories at first-floor level. The buildings were converted into flats, but the remains of the balconies that linked up all the houses can still be seen.

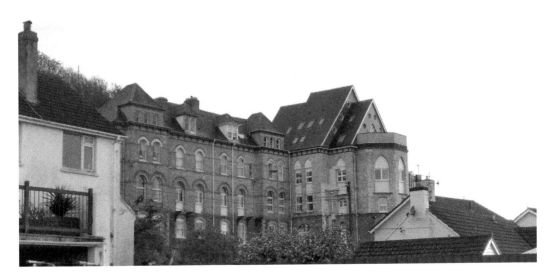

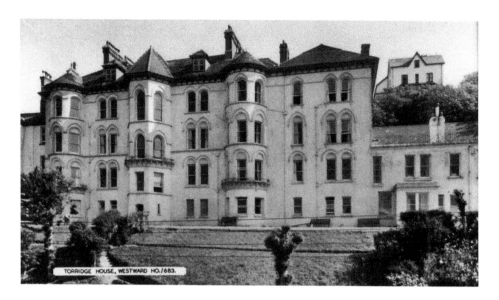

TORRIDGE HOUSE, WESTWARD HO./683.

Torridge House

Captain G. Molesworth built several large villas in the new Westward Ho!, such as Rowena and Torridge House in Kingsley Road. He retired from the Navy aged only thirty-three and after only nine years' service, and was probably given the title of 'Captain' by his golfing friends. He was lucky enough to marry Sarah Newall, an extremely rich cotton heiress from Manchester, and the money to develop Westward Ho! came from his fortuitous marriage. They lived in Cliff House, Limers Lane in Northam, where he ran the lime kiln and had a brick-making business. He used a chalet in the Riversford Hotel gardens as his business office. In Westward Ho! he built the Bath House Hotel and Nassau Baths, the gasworks, started United Services College and Kingsley College. His idea for Torridge House was to build it as a sanatorium, but it later became an upmarket guest house. In 1868, it was announced that the German Chancellor Bismarck was taking over the house for the summer. He advertised it as fashionable boarding for private families and golfers opposite the Union Club. Highgate School was evacuated here in the war but later it was taken over by the Army and became the headquarters of COXE. Now Torridge House is split up into apartments and called Kingsley Court.

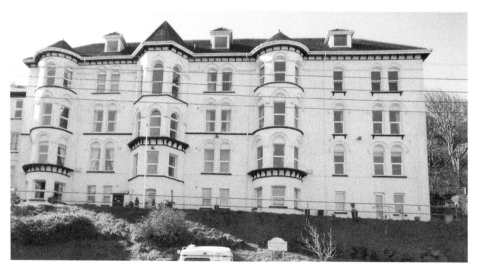

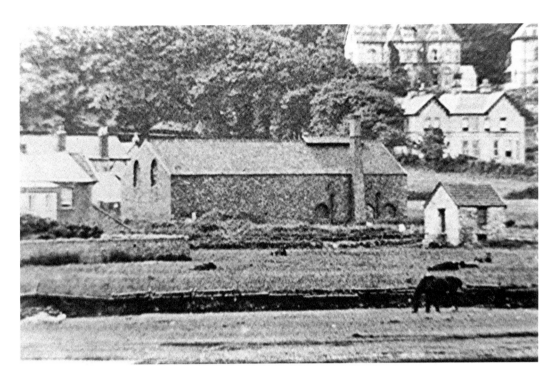

Old Gasworks. Avon Lane

Rudyard Kipling, who was at school at the United Services College, wrote his novel *Stalky and Co.* based on his experiences there: 'One windy winter's night Stalky ... turned a key and ... the lights of the Coastguard Cottages went out, the brilliantly lit windows of the Golf Club disappeared and were followed by the frontage of the two hotels, scattered villas dulled, twinkled and vanished. Last of all the College lights died also. They were left in pitchy darkness.' He had turned off Molesworth's gasometer in the wood just above the college.

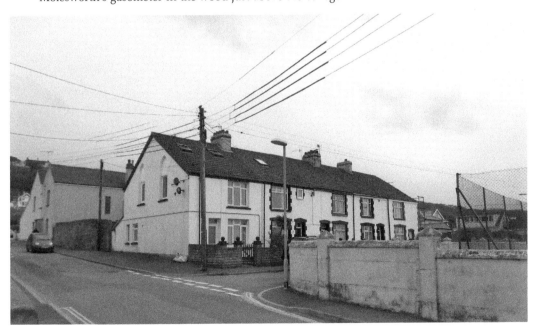

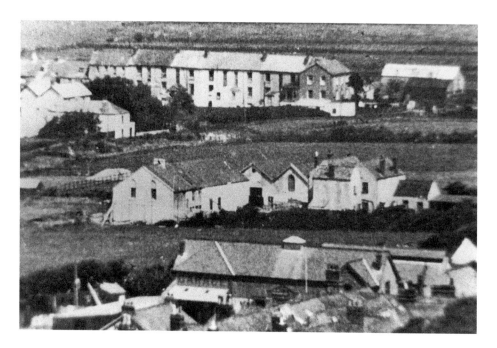

Old Gasworks, Avon Lane

The old gasworks is in the left foreground with its chimney and arched windows still there today, though now it's converted into a row of cottages. The railway had a siding to it for delivery of coal. Eastbourne Terrace runs from left to right along the back of the picture, and Avon Lane runs from left to right in the foreground. Aysha House, then called Marine Villa, is in the middle of the photograph with its castellated tower, and this house was also requisitioned for Highgate School. The gasworks had a circular gas holder here and also piped gas up to another gas holder in the woods at the side of Fosketh Hill, where the foundations remain to this day. The Avon Lane gasworks remain too, converted to a row of cottages still with the imprints of those arched windows.

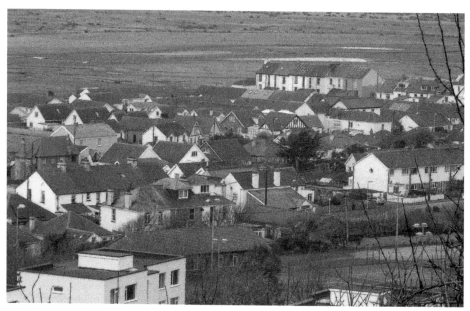

Old Post Office, No. 1, Nelson Terrace, c. 1914
Here is the old post office in Nelson Terrace with its ornate windows. The postmaster, Lt-Cmdr Newcombe, proudly holds his little granddaughter with his wife behind him. The family brought the post office here from a house called Campden further along the road, now called Golden Sands Nursing Home. The shop window signs advertise 'Three styles of cigarettes, Lyons Tea and Cadbury's Cocoa'.

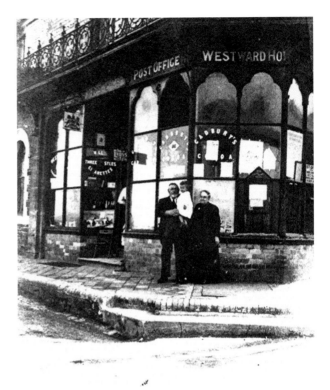

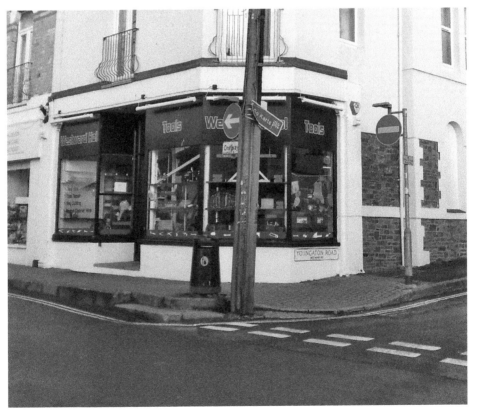

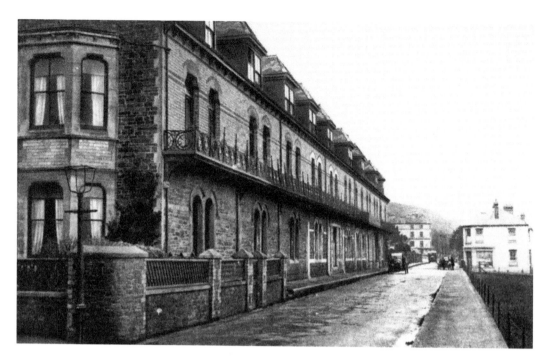

Nelson Terrace

An early photograph of Nelson Terrace with only peaceful fields of sheep on the right-hand side and no houses or shops built here yet. Later there was to be a tennis court to the right, which became the first small tennis club at Westward Ho! before the house called Glenburnie, now the post office, was built on it. Only five houses were originally built in Nelson Terrace, and the remaining four were constructed later by a different builder. The elegant cast-iron balconies are now sadly gone, though the rose decorations are still there. No. 1 at the far end was a bakery with ovens in the cellar in 1871 and it became the tuck shop for the USC boys who were kept so short of food at school. By 1881, this shop was the post office.

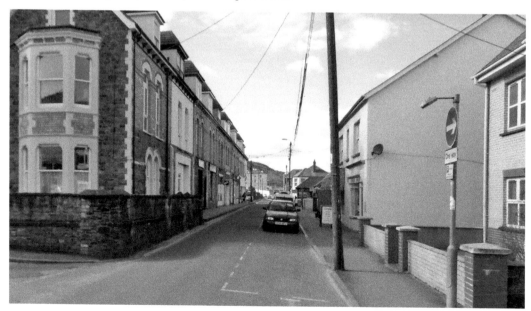

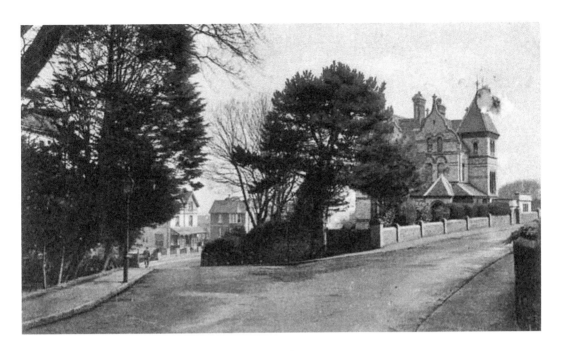

Junction of Atlantic Way and Golf Links Road
This old photograph shows a peaceful, picturesque, tree-lined scene, but the trees have now gone and the roads have been widened. Ferndale is to the right with pointed tower and The Chalet is to the left in the distance. The *Bideford Gazette* of 1878 described Ferndale as 'beautifully situated with splendid views of the Golf Links, complete accommodation for a family with walled flower garden and croquet lawn built in Gothic style'. Later Ferndale became The Ship public house until converted to apartments and extended carefully to match the original architectural style; it then reverted to its original name of Ferndale.

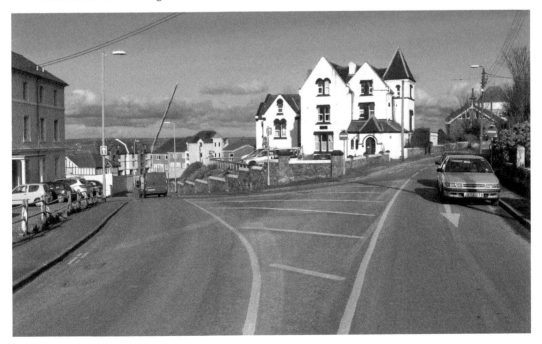

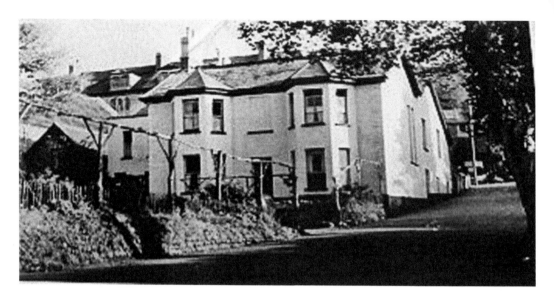

Youngaton Farm House, Now The Village Inn

The old Youngaton Farm is much older than Westward Ho! itself and was the only farm in the immediate vicinity of the village, then called Underborough and Western Youngaton. The three original farms were Youngaton, Underborough and Venton. In 1423, during the reign of Henry VI, George Cole gave all his land and tenements at Underborough to the religious guild at Northam, but later the guild was confiscated and passed to Thomas Collimore. Thomas Leigh then bought the confiscated land at Underborough and Youngaton back, but granted annuities or rent to the parish instead. In 1656, its owner John Beaple gave £5 to the poor of Northam from his messuage and tenement of West Youngaton and Underborough. Like so many other houses, it was requisitioned in the Second World War and used as a sanatorium for Highgate School, which was evacuated here and took over so many of Westward Ho!'s buildings. Later it became Grenville public house and is now called The Village Inn.

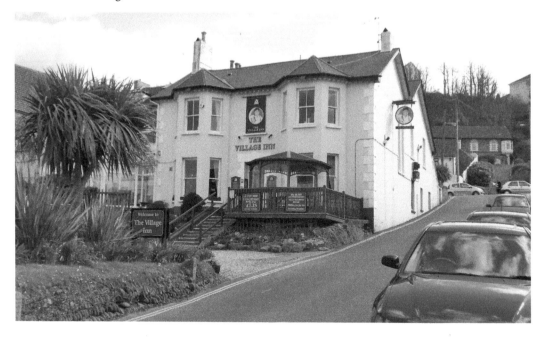

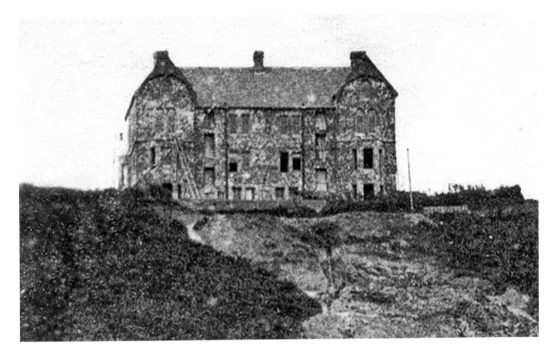

Edgehill, Bay View Road, Being Built

The Junior School of the United Services College started in a house at Buckleigh in 1879 with only fifteen boys. After only five terms it relocated to this house in Bay View Road on the hillside just above the college in 1880. Edgehill had previously been used just for the very youngest boys aged from six to nine years before the junior school moved back to Buckleigh Place. This interesting old photograph shows Edgehill actually in the process of being built, with its empty unglazed windows, a builder's ladder propped against the wall and the garden unmade.

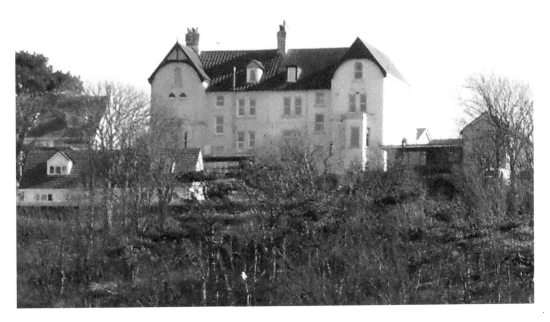

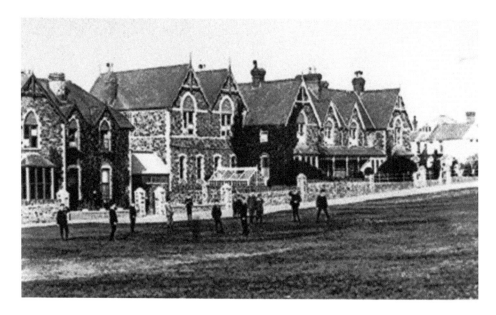

College Close

These four houses were the only ones in College Close when the junior department of USC moved down from Edgehill in Bay View Road and took them over in 1882. Romantically, they were called San Rosa and Rose Cottage, Richmond Villa and Rose Bank – how the Victorians loved their Rose names! As had been done in all three schools, they were combined by a corridor and linking buildings and they became the school – though the water supply proved temperamental at times! The picture shows the linking corridors between the houses and the boys playing outside. It was an excellent site for a school and advertised itself as 'preparing boys from seven to fourteen years of age for the navy and public schools, surrounded by its own playing fields of 5 acres and situated 200 feet above sea level on a hill. The climate is bracing and invigorating and particularly suited to boys inclined to delicacy. Electric light throughout. Bathing daily in the seas.' The school constructed a footpath down through the wood, for ease of access between the two schools and for sea bathing, which is still there.

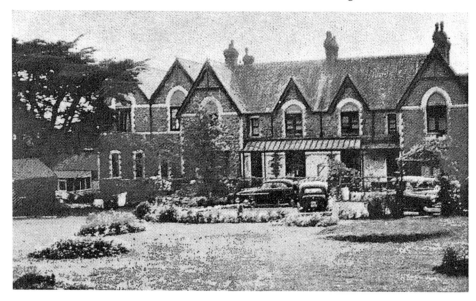

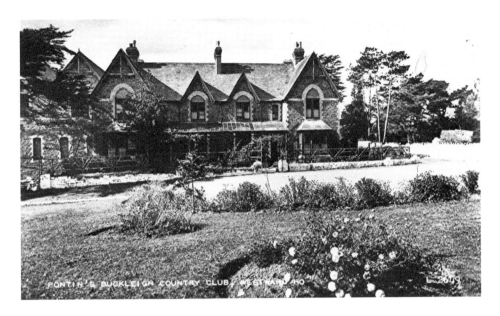

College Close After the Junior School

During the war, Highgate School took over the whole of the site for their evacuation here, including Bellevue Hotel, which was later renamed Buckleigh Grange and is now a small estate. In 1947, the four houses and the school site became a Pontins Holiday Camp called the Buckleigh Place Country Club and the dormitories became holiday accommodation; the school hall became a ballroom. A heated swimming pool was added in 1964, which is still used by local residents. In 1972 the whole site was sold to property developers, who demolished the two original houses on the left, which had contained the ballroom and the kitchen area, and built two blocks of flats on the site. The old dormitories in the other two houses were also turned into apartments.

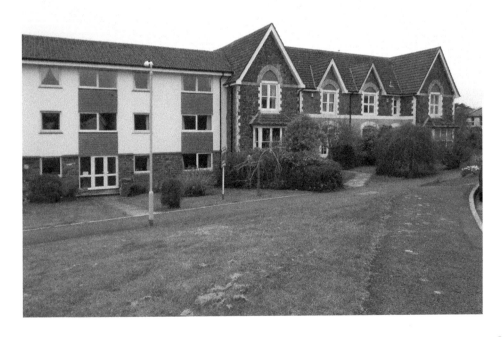

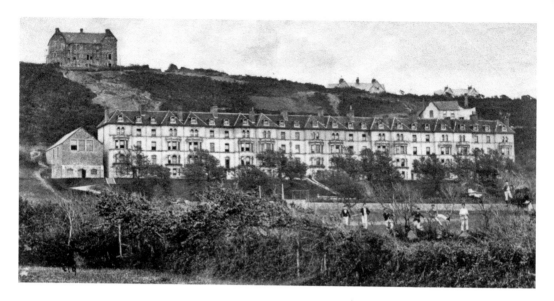

United Services College, Kingsley Terrace, Founded 1874

An early photograph with only Edgehill on the skyline in Bay View Road. Boys from USC are sitting on a bank in their playing field in front of their school. The school laundry is just above the college rooftops on the right with its chimney showing prominently. The hillside was once used as grazing land but is now thickly covered in trees. Once called United Services Proprietary College, it took over the whole of Kingsley Terrace; however, its information said 'though ample accommodation for 200 boys, it is hoped that this edifice may form only the junior school to a more extensive establishment to be built upon ground near the same spot' – ambitious indeed! It went on to report that the new gymnasium is completed and they proposed to erect a fives court. The school was intended to provide sons of officers with a public school education at lower cost than could be obtained elsewhere.

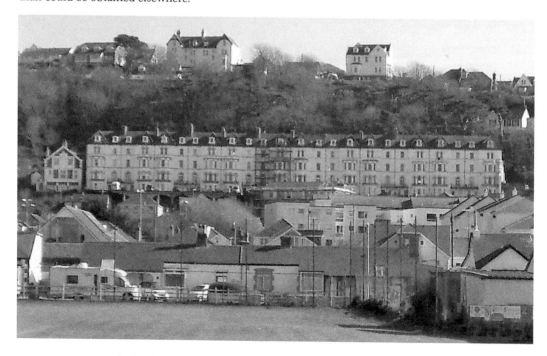

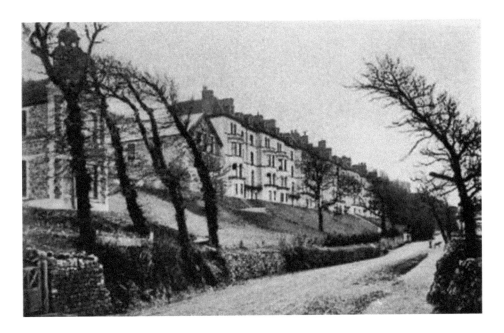

United Services College

Molesworth built twelve terraced houses, later renamed Kipling Terrace as boarding houses. By the time the school was planned, they were for sale cheaply and the school took over the whole terrace and ran a corridor through from end to end. USC had a chapel to the left of the college in the picture. The college was always short of money and the school meals were sparse and plain. Breakfast was only bread and butter and coffee served from a pewter urn. For an extra fee, potatoes and a small plate of sausages were allowed. Midday dinner was roast meat and boiled vegetables, a pudding and small beer. Evening tea was bread and coffee again, served with a hunk of cheese. Unfortunately, the cooked meals were horribly tainted by the taste and smell of gas from the primitive gas ovens. No wonder that the boys were only too glad to go down to the post office to buy a bun thickly spread with jam and clotted cream.

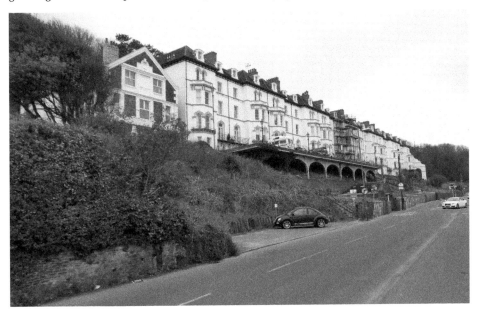

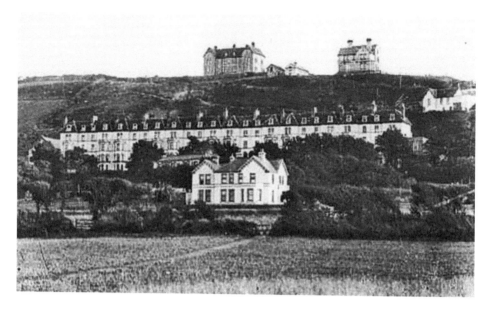

Lost Road to Westward Ho!

Up on the skyline on Bay View Road there are only two houses yet – Edgehill and Hillcliff – but the old Link House is in the foreground with United Services College behind it. This is a very rare photograph that clearly shows the very old original main road into Westward Ho!, now long gone, which is to be seen running down the treeless hillside diagonally from the skyline in Bay View Road to pass in front of the old United Services College laundry (upper right edge) to join up with Fosketh Hill. This old road ran from Abbotsham to Silford Cross and then bore to the right along the lane, crossing the fields to emerge onto Bay View Road at almost its highest point. Having crossed over Bay View Road, it diverged into two old roads which led precipitously downwards, west to Westward Ho! long before the village was even thought of and east to Northam Burrows.

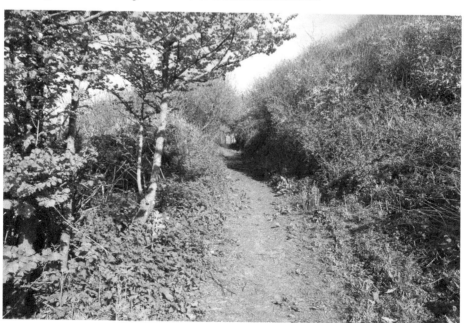

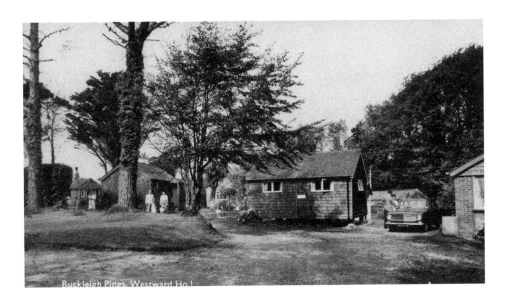

Buckleigh Pines, Westward Ho !

Buckleigh Pines Holiday Camp

Cornborough Road was once a huge clifftop holiday centre overlooking the bay with a series of tent and caravan parks. Before the time of package holidays abroad using air travel, many families took their holidays at British seaside resorts in gigantic holiday camps run on an industrial scale. Once there, many never left the campsite for the whole of their fortnight's stay, with all meals and entertainment and competitions laid on. The camps were low cost, people being housed in quite basic wooden chalets as in the picture here. All the camps on Cornborough Road have long since gone, to be replaced by housing estates. In the lower picture, the entrance to the camp is still there, leading to a house that was once the camp shop, and the last of the Buckleigh pine trees is still in the garden.

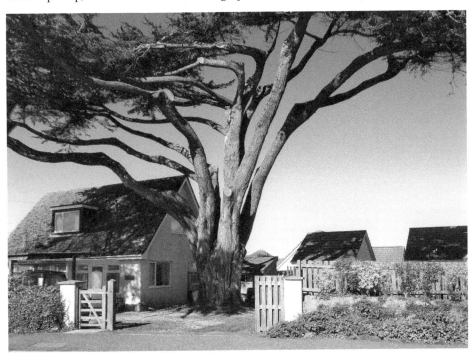

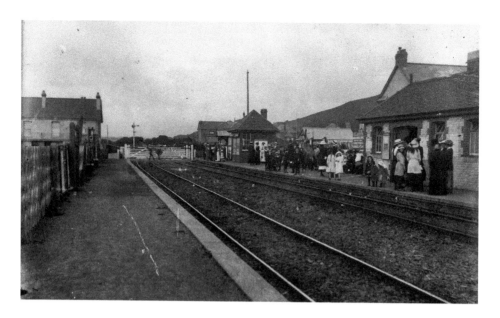

Westward Ho! Station, Looking East, c. 1910.

The station was of a very respectable size for such a small railway. It had a waiting room, a buffet, a bookstall, a signal box, a passing loop and two platforms. In 1903, a 'Reception Hall for concerts, dances and other entertainments, and shelter for bad weather' was built and called Station Hall. The building on the right of the photograph was the waiting room, which was converted into a bungalow after the railway closed, but later demolished. The little square building with the pointed roof was the signal box. The station seems busy here, with several parties of schoolchildren waiting to board the train. Large quantities of coal were transported through here on the way to the railway gasworks siding just past the level crossing in the distance. After the line closed, the station site became the bus terminus for a time, the signal box became a café and the station hall remained in use as a dance hall and then became the Buccaneer Inn, but it has all been demolished and redeveloped as Latitude 51.

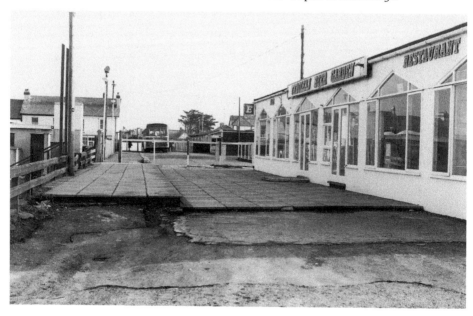

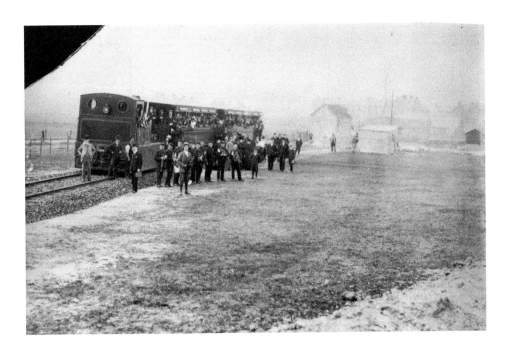

Avon Lane Halt, 1901

This halt was almost at the junction of Avon Lane and Golf Links Road, on the site of the present-day council-owned tennis courts. The photograph looks across the end of Avon Lane with Eastbourne Terrace and Aysha House, then called Marine Villa, in the background. At the time of the old photograph a man lived in the barn on the left of the group of buildings, sleeping in the hayloft upstairs and keeping his horse and dray downstairs. Just to the right of the picture, a siding ran to the old gasworks and the route of the line is still clearly evident through the main car park at Westward Ho! today.

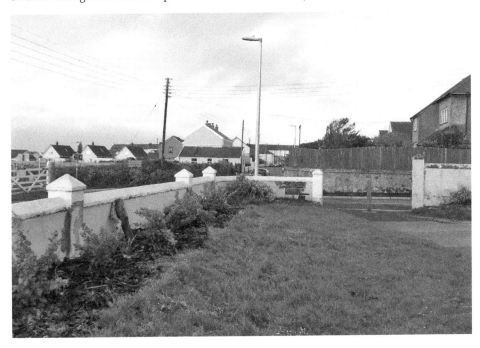

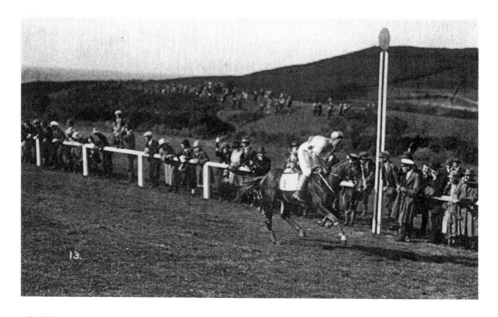

Shebbertown Racecourse

The new racecourse was opened in September 1922 at Abbotsham Cliffs and was described by Tatler as 'the most beautifully situated race course in England' as it ran along the valley towards the sea. It opened to great acclaim and 'dozens of motor char-a-bancs and motor cars turned up to watch the first races' with accompanying music. A grandstand was planned but never built as the racecourse, badly overlooked by public footpaths, never paid its way, and the public soon realised that paying for tickets was not necessary. Little is left on the cliffs today, though the entrance gates and entrance road built on the old Abbotsham Road railway line remain, as do the former refreshment rooms and clubhouse near the top entrance, which was later converted to a bungalow.

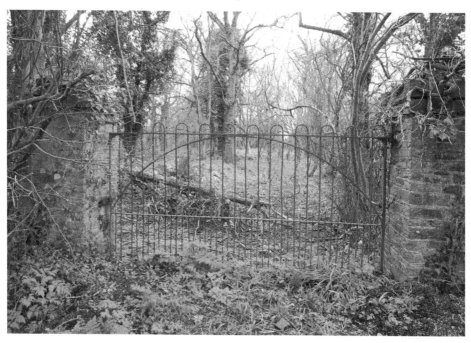

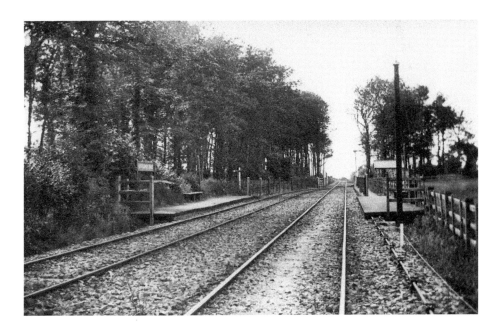

Abbotsham Road Station, Looking North

The photographer is standing looking towards the sea. The level crossing across the Cornborough Road was just ahead beyond the station here, with the main line on the right and the loop line on the left. Both lines have their own platforms with passenger walkways along to the level crossing. The more distant part of the line has now been ploughed out and has disappeared completely in the field, but the nearer part runs into the wood on the left of the photograph and is still there as a low embankment. On the further side of the level crossing there are some large gates, which were put in place after the demise of the railway as an entrance to the old racecourse on the cliffs, but this entranceway was laid on the old line and the level crossing gate pillars can still be found there.

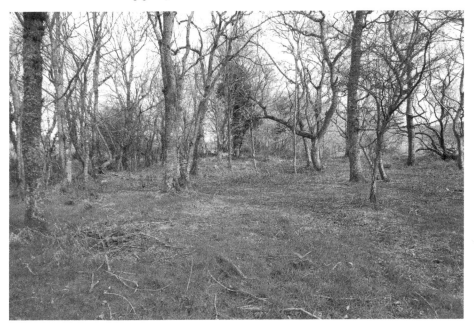

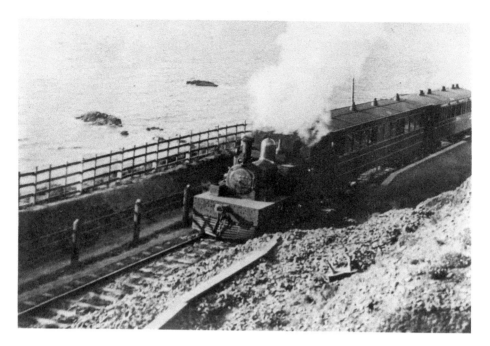

Cornborough Cliffs Halt, 1915

Cornborough Halt was the last halt before the train ran on along the cliffs and down into the Westward Ho! station. The halt platform seen on the right of the photograph was 30 feet long but only 6 inches high, and accessed by a footpath seen on the left. The track along the cliffs was cut through the rock and is still well defined when approached from the footpath past Seafield House. The train stopped here only by request, mostly by people wanting to walk on the Tors. This is *Torridge* on its journey back to Bideford pulling a first class carriage and then a composite coach with both first and third class seats (there was no second class). The railway opened in 1911 and closed in 1917.

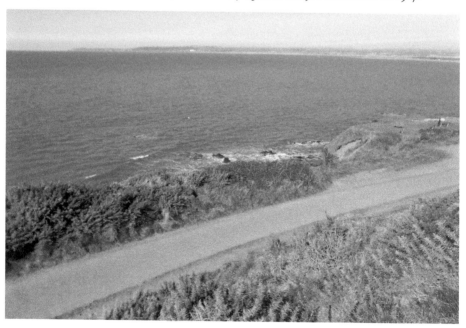

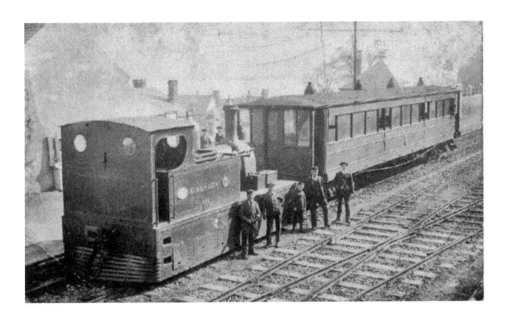

The End of the Railway

The Northam, Westward Ho! & Appledore Railway always struggled to pay its way, and by 1914 the accounts showed serious losses. Passengers from Bideford station had to walk over the bridge to take the train whose onward journey was 7 miles by rail, yet only 3 miles by road. Mr Dymond ran horse buses frequently and tickets were cheaper and journeys faster. By 1914 people were giving up holidays because of the war, there was a shortage of labour to run the railway when workers were requisitioned, and finally the engines were requisitioned too. The last trains ran in March 1917, the three engines were taken across Bideford Bridge to the station and the carriages left in the sheds at Bideford to await the reopening, which never happened. Finally, in 1921 the carriages were auctioned off and advertised as having teak wood bodies and lit with acetylene gas. Several were cut into sections. One became a beach hut in the sandhills, some were used as farm huts and piggeries like the one below.

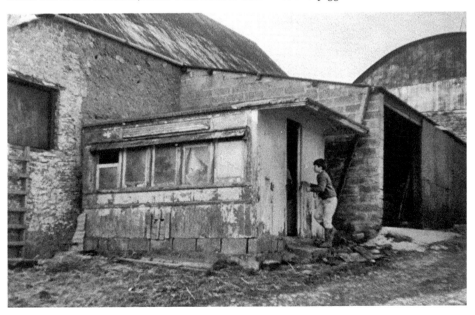

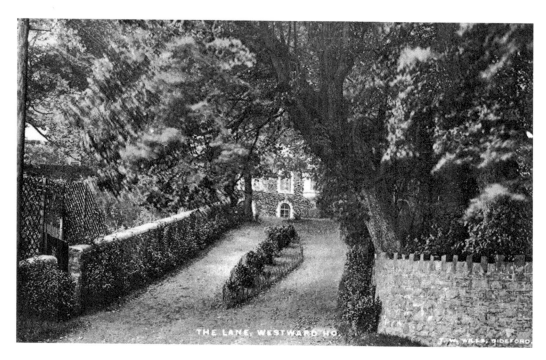

THE LANE, WESTWARD HO.

The Lane/May Hilder Way

Known as The Lane at this time, this pretty and peaceful road was the middle section of the ancient packhorse route down to the sea. Originally called Long Lane, it began up on Bay View Road by Upper Lodge, came down Fosketh Hill, then down this lane and on down past Youngaton Inn, which was a farm, and finally down Youngaton Road and Station Road to the seashore. The old livery stables belonging to the house called Rowena can be seen at the top of the lane here.

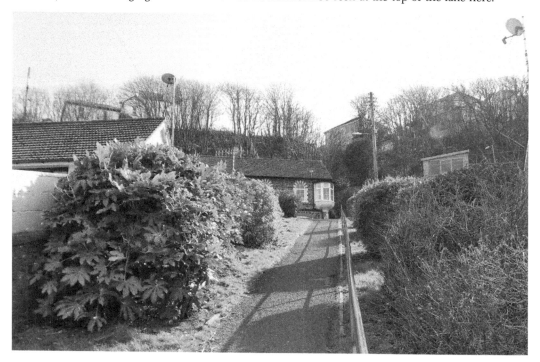

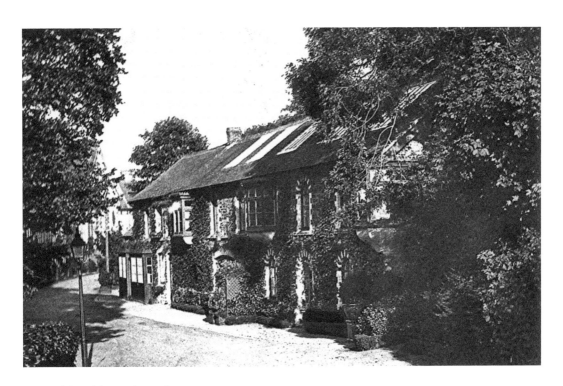

Old Stables and Coach House. *c.* 1920
The coach house and stables were built in 1871 to provide livery stables and to house the coaches for visitors to the sanatorium at Torridge House and the hotel at Rowena. In 1901, the stable premises on the left of the coach house were built to add to the first building. At this time the building was covered in creepers and the street is attractively tree lined and has a gas lamp. The old stables are now called Bracken House.

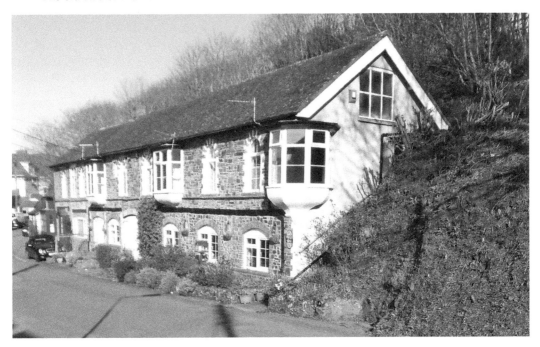

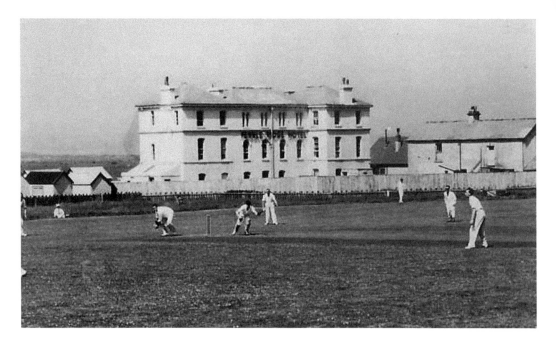

Pebbleridge Hotel

Thomas Pynsent, one of the directors of the Westward Ho! Company, built Pebbleridge Hotel, which opened in 1865, a few days before the Royal Hotel. It was described as a first-class lodging house, furnished and carpeted in the best style suitable for picnic parties, and with stabling for twelve horses. It was built only 100 yards from the pebble ridge. Later it was divided into apartments, deteriorated, was attacked by vandals and became derelict. Eventually a fire gutted the inside and it was burned down in August 1993. The fire was so intense that firemen from Bideford, Appledore and Ilfracombe had to remain outside to fight the fire and the roof collapsed. For some time afterwards it was left as a pile of rubble until the site was cleared and bungalows built.

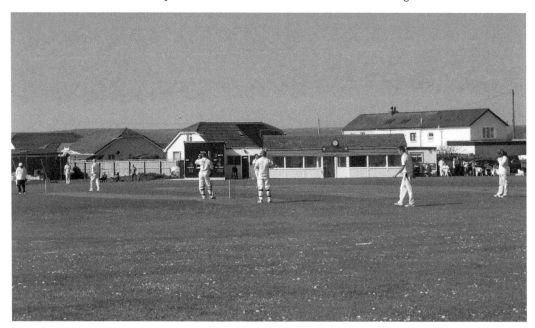

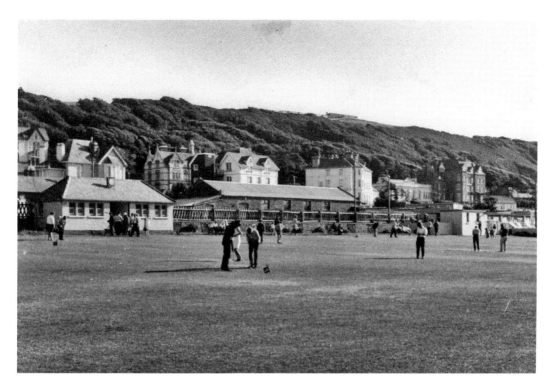

Westward Ho! Village Green

The earlier green was set out for putting, with several flower beds, and also had weather shelters that offered the opportunity to get out of the wind. Over the last two decades, the area has been transformed into a village green where holidaymakers can lounge on the grass and watch the world go by. The brass bands still play here in summer, and it is now surrounded by very modern-style apartments and café/restaurants.

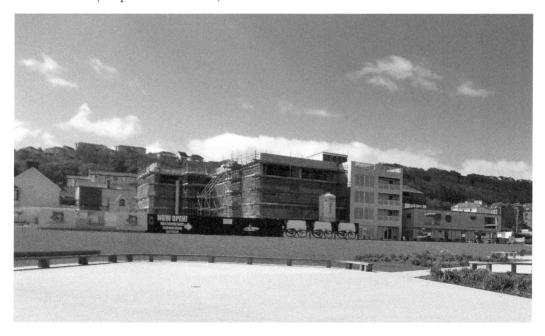

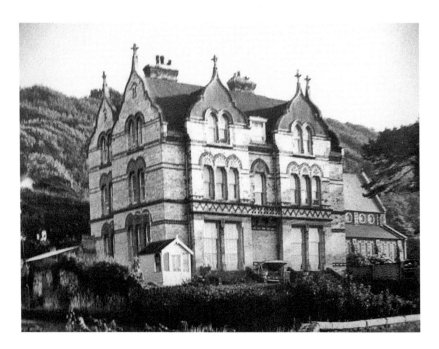

Ferndale

This was once the most decorative and picturesque mansion in Westward Ho!, with its Gothic styling, beautiful gable ends, decorative brickwork and string courses. Here it is in its gracious heyday, with spreading lawns, summerhouse, luxurious roofed swing seat, croquet lawn and walled flower garden. Its descent from grace was precipitous when it became The Ship public house, its attractive brickwork plastered over, and its gable ends changed to utilitarian style. In 2005, it was renovated and extended sympathetically to blend in with the old part, converted to flats and it reverted to its original name of Ferndale.

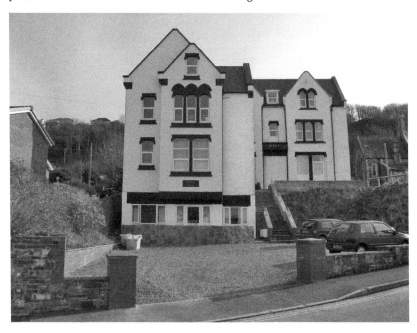

Northam

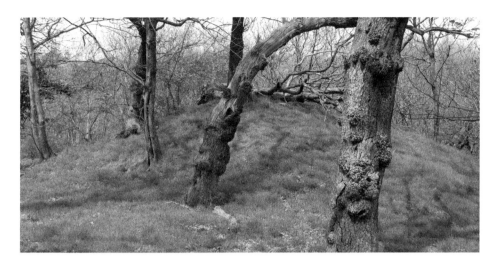

Godborough and Kenwith Castles

Kenwith and Godborough Castles are strange, mysterious earthworks whose origins have been lost in the mists of time. That there was a battle at 'Arx Cynuit' between the Danes and the native Anglo-Saxons is not in doubt, and local tradition avows that it was here, with Cynuit sounding so similar to Kenwith. Tradition also has it that the Danes came ashore at Boat Hyde and set up camp at Godborough, with the defending Odda at Kenwith. Almost 800 Danes were slaughtered, including their leader, Hubba. Godborough has been visited several times by archaeologists in the last thirty years to survey the site. The fort is 320 metres by 190 metres with an enclosure within the fort of 80 metres by 30 metres, raised in the east to give a good viewpoint. There are also some strange excavations here, as yet undefined. Was this a moat, water collection for the army stationed here, or maybe coal mining exploration? Also of great interest is a large wall and dyke running south-east from the camp right down to the valley floor.

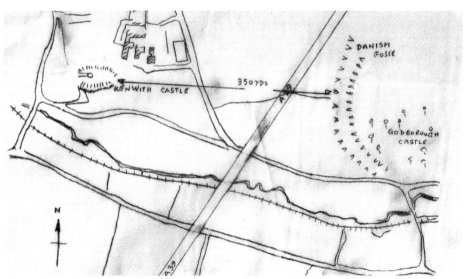

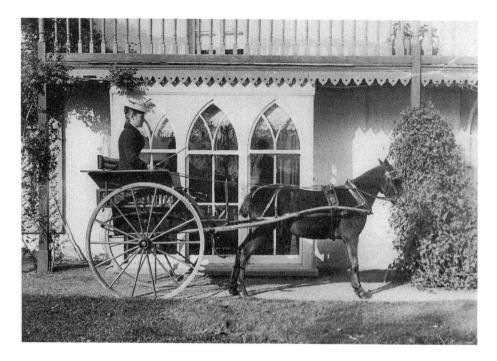

Boat Hyde, 1898

Boat Hyde is a very old site and referred to as Bothythe in 1397. Built on the River Torridge, it was originally just an old farmhouse and, like Hyde Barton, was approached via Windmill Lane, which was called Hyde Lane then (Hyde is derived from the Old English word *hyo* – a landing place). The lane also led down to a very early ford, which was one of the two ancient crossing places before Bideford Bridge was built, and also to an old limekiln on the river, which is still there. The lime kiln was romanticised into a mock castle by the Victorians. The original Boat Hyde was just a two-up-two-down farmhouse, which faced the creek where the tide rushed in twice a day before the two levees were built.

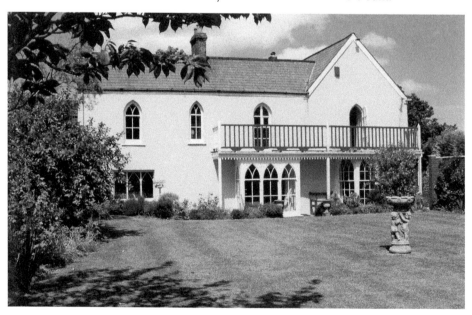

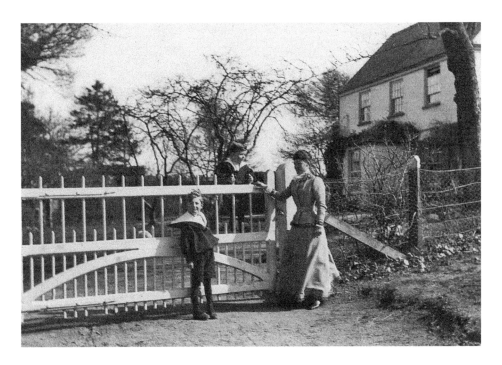

Boat Hyde, 1898

There were shipyards at the bottom of the garden on the river and a railway line ran along the inner levee to the Marley brick and tile works on the site of the present Bidna shipyard. Like so many other large houses, Boat Hyde was requisitioned in the First World War and the Ministry of Agriculture housed a vet here and installed the first phone in the village for him, giving him the very first telephone number – Northam 1! There were no mains services here till the 1950s; water was pumped up from the well in the old farmyard to a huge lead tank in the roof, and gas for lighting was made by dripping water onto calcium carbide to make acetylene gas. The Nixon family, who had come from Ireland with their racehorses, are pictured.

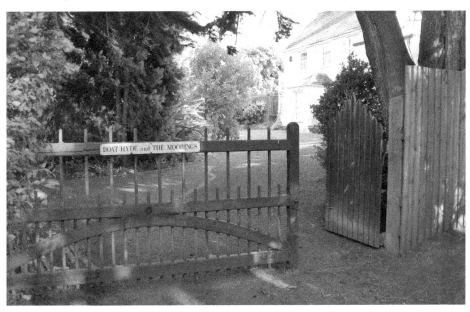

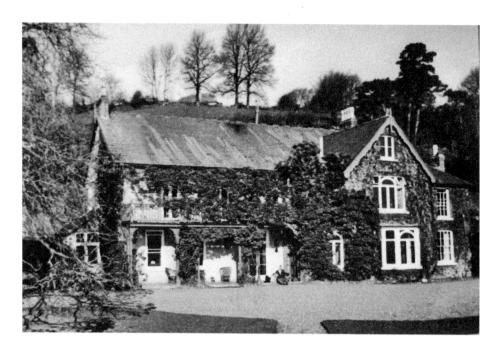

Cleave Barton

The north end of Cleave was entirely separated from the south end by the tidal estuary and there was once no road connection. The only access to this south end began in Goats Hill Road, and diverged from it on the right down the old disused lane that connected Goats Hill Road with Clevelands Park. Halfway down was another drive to the big house, Clevelands. The road down to Cleave went on down Clevelands Park from there and along the old track to the lodge house to Cleave Barton. From here it went on down to the estuary where there was once an old tide mill. Cleave Barton was a large mansion but was extended and divided into three separate houses some years ago. In 1906 it was advertised in an auction as the 'perfect abode for sportsmen and golfers, anchorage for any size yachts, private landing quay, clad in wisteria and creepers [as shown in the photograph] and with eleven bed and dressing rooms, stabling, lodge house, vinery and orchards'.

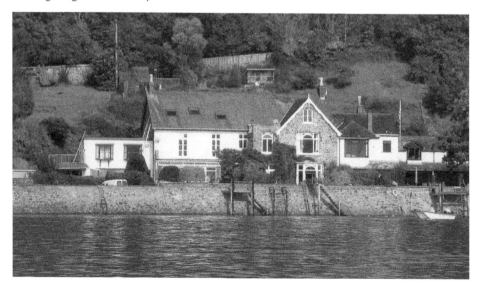

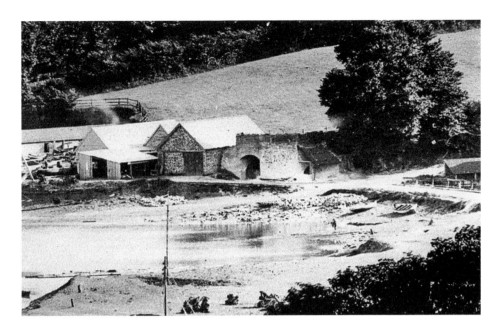

Old Lime Kiln at Cleave

We are at the bottom of Limers Lane, looking back from the river at the lime kiln here. This was once the industrial centre of Northam, with a lime kiln, brick and tile making works to its left, and boatbuilding yards all along the river. There was even a quarry here, with a little railway track bringing the stone down to the river's edge to load into boats on the river. Limers Lane was once called Riversford Lane after an earlier ford across the Torridge here. At the time of the photograph, there was no road connecting the two ends of Cleave and the little quarry line came down between the two ends and the river came right up to the wall. This peaceful stretch of the river was once a hive of activity, with boats and barges laden with coal and lime for the kiln floating up the river on the high tide, the brick kilns working, the noise from the quarry and the hammering from the boat builders. In earlier times, there was also a tide mill at the other end of Cleave. Access to the other end was only via Durrant Lane or along Goats Hill Road.

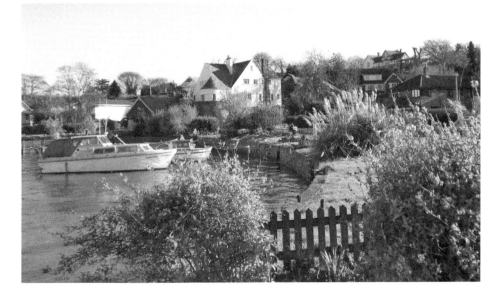

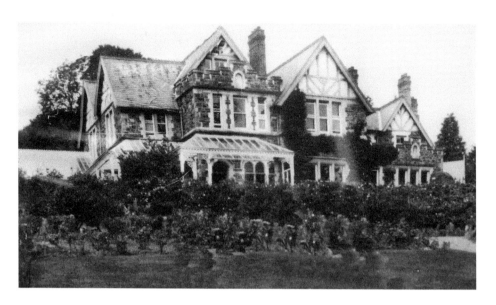

Yeolden House

Although there was already an old farmhouse here called Clyffe Farm, shown on the old maps of the time, Yeolden House was built in its present form in around 1860, when the old farmhouse was assimilated into the present building. From the fourteenth century there was a shipyard at the bottom of the garden called Chapman's Yard, which adjoined the river at that time. Drake's fire ships for his 1587 expedition were reputedly constructed here. The river wall was built by Napoleonic French prisoners of war and the shipyard moved then. By 1911, Mrs Dawe owned the house with a staff of six inside servants, three gardeners, a coachman, and her 5 acres of beautiful gardens and tennis court were regularly opened to the public. With the names of so many houses in the neighbourhood variants of Cliff, Cleeve, Cleavelands, she decided to rename the house Yeolden. In her time, water was pumped up to a roof holding tank from the well and the house was lit by acetylene gas. In 1917, Mrs Dawe changed her carriage horses, Lightning and Starlight, for one of the first motor cars in the area and took on a chauffeur instead of a coachman. In 1947 the house was converted to an hotel and one of the guests stayed on for twenty-three years! It has been a much loved and popular hotel ever since.

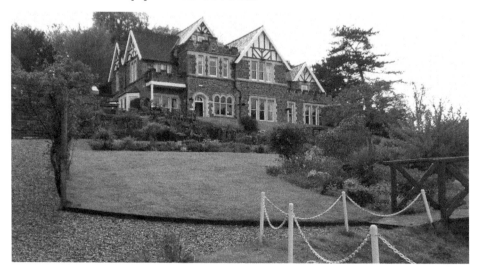

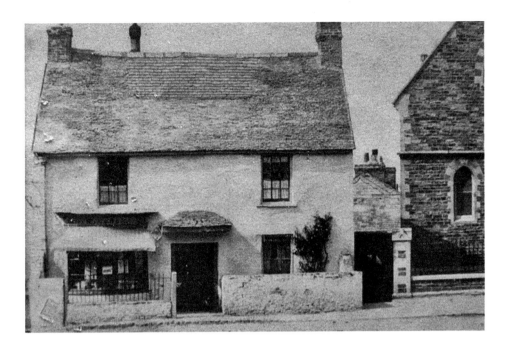

Northam Square

The old cottage in the middle of the picture was once an inn called The Ringers' Inn. At other times it has been a bakery, a greengrocer, a grocery and quite recently the main post office. This early photograph shows it as a shop in the front room of the cottage. At present it is a garden shop. To the left of the old cottage is New Causeway Hill. Once this was even narrower than it is now, as there were two more cottages obscuring the entrance to the road that have now been demolished. At one time, the main road to Appledore was via Honey Street, where there was a coaching inn, and then through Oxmans Lane and Lewis Hill. New Causeway Hill didn't exist at this time, but was eventually built up to become the main road to Appledore to take wheeled traffic.

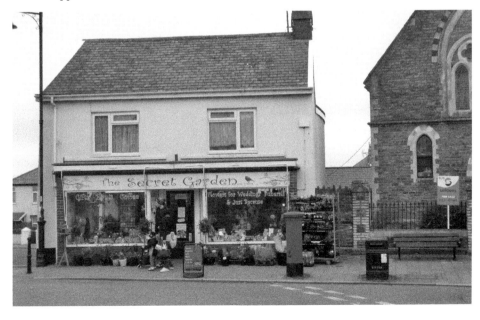

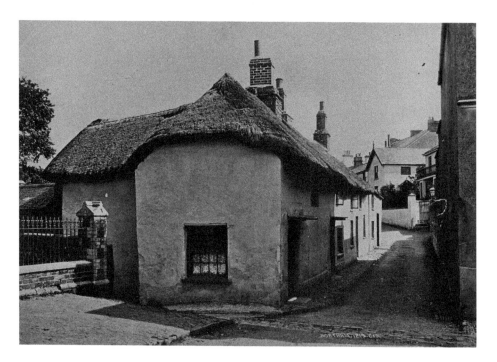

Junction of North Street and Northam Square

The railings of the old Congregational chapel on the left have now been converted to flats, and the old thatched cottages in the centre of picture have now also been replaced by modern houses. The schoolchildren used the room under the chapel as their lunch room, which during the war became a British restaurant (originally called Communal Feeding Centres). These were set up for people who had been bombed out, and provided food very cheaply for the general public and war workers. Before the chapel was built, there was a gateway to a farm here.

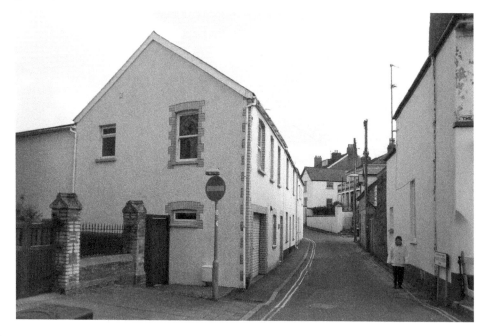

Mr Jones' Cycle Shop, Fore Street, c. 1910

This was the great age of the bicycle – at last ordinary people had access to some transport! Mr Jones advertises Raleigh cycles. The photograph is carefully posed with the owner and his wife outside in her best dress, his shield advertising cycles propped up, and several little boys getting into the picture. Many village houses at this time had a wide access at the side of the house through to the backyard for ease of access for a horse, or for a pig or two ,which were often kept domestically, fattened on household scraps and then butchered for family consumption. There is a hayloft above with a full length door. This shop later became a newspaper shop. On the right of the shop, the old vestry building still has its external stone steps, which were later removed. On the left is the entrance to the King's Head Hotel stables and motor garage.

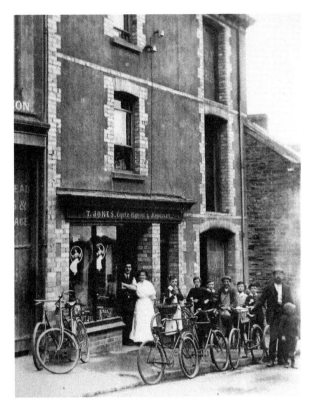

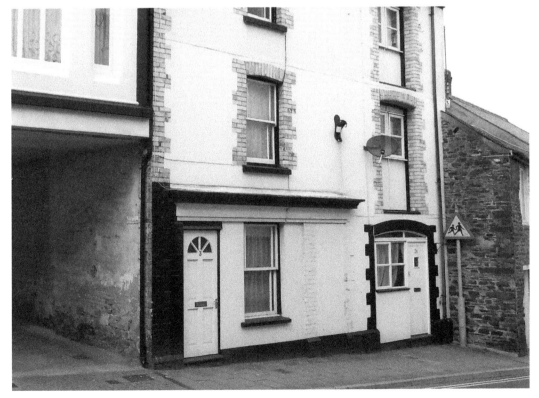

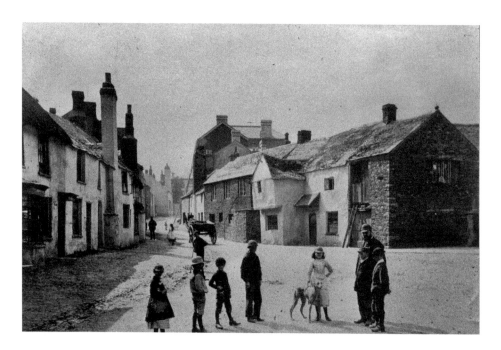

Northam Square, 1880s and 1960

Northam Square always seems to have been an open space and a wide street for the May Fair and a market. In the 1880s, Mr Jones' paper shop was just a farm linhay with a ladder up to the first storey. At this time, the old Vestry Room had a stone-built outside staircase, which had been removed by the time of the later photograph. This building was once a charity school with the under room used as the Northam lock-up to hold prisoners temporarily when en route to Exeter gaol. By 1960, today's supermarket (on the left of the two photographs) was a garage and filling station, where 'accumulators' could also be charged; these were lead acid batteries used to run people's radios and older type telephones. The garage also had a small area for new cars to be exhibited and had petrol pumps on the pavement edge.

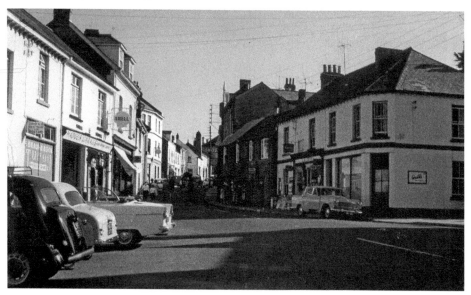

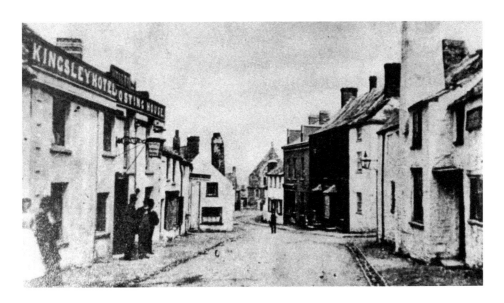

Old Kingsley Hotel, Fore Street, Northam, c. 1880

A very early photograph of Fore Street when the pavements were cobbled and the street just a dried earth track. The old Kingsley Hotel on the left advertises itself as a posting house, where horses were kept so that a fresh relay of horses could be exchanged for the next stage of the journey, or rested and fed overnight and travellers could be accommodated. Sadly, it burned down in 1917 and had to be rebuilt, but this is a photograph of the original Kingsley Hotel with men outside in their top hats and hotel maids in long dresses. The night of the fire was so cold that the water froze into icicles on the firemen's tunics. It's hard to remember that this was the main road to Appledore before the Northam bypass was built. Traffic turned right here to proceed along narrow Cross Street and there was even a policeman stationed here on point duty (seen in the photograph) to direct the light flow of traffic. The old-fashioned signpost on the telegraph pole directs traffic to turn right to Appledore and another sign points to the post office, which was also in Cross Street at this time. On the left are the two hotels side by side – first the Kingsley and then the King's Head Hotel.

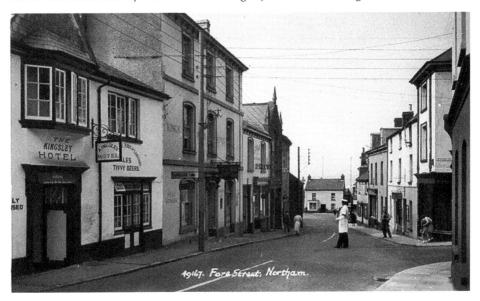

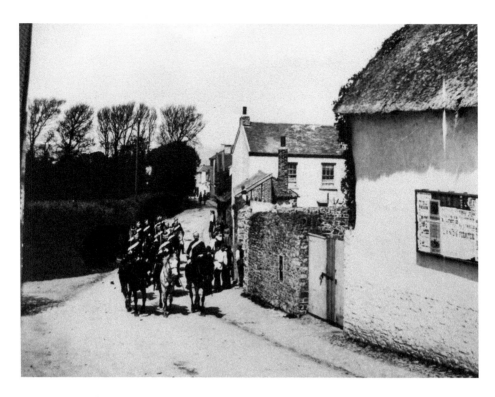

The Upper End of Fore Street, Northam, 1905, and Snowy Scene, 1950
We are looking down Fore Street from the top and the North Devon Hussars are trotting back up the street after their annual camp at Commons Farm. They are just approaching the entrance to Dymond's horse-drawn carriages stable. The stables, which are thatched in the upper picture, are still there in the later picture but have now been demolished, though the old wall on to the road remains to this day and new houses have been built on the site. Both photographs show Bay View Road (Cross Lane as it was then called) coming in on the left as both predate the building of the Northam bypass. The house with Georgian windows looking on to Fore Street is called Lyalls, though in 1820 it was the Hunters' Inn.

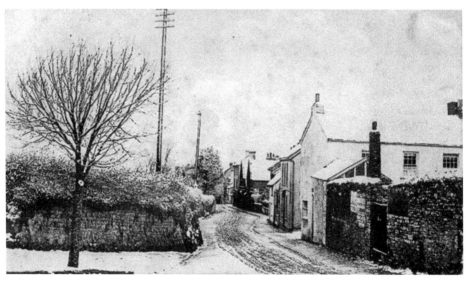

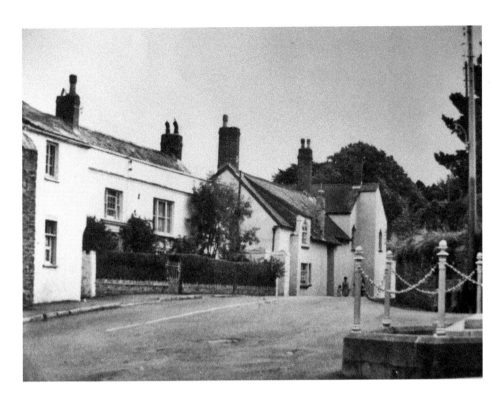

Cross House, Fore Street, Northam

Cross House is a listed eighteenth-century two-storey house at the top of the village. It was once used as a farm and later associated with Dymond's stables, which operated from the site next door. Behind the house there were gardens, orchards and stables, and this large area of land became the site of Fox Hole estate when it was built on this land in 1971. There are the usual village rumours of an underground passage running to the church that many old mansions seem to collect, though this house may have had some sort of link to the church (hence its name). Bay View Road opposite the house was once known as Cross Lane, but it is unclear whether the house name or street name is older.

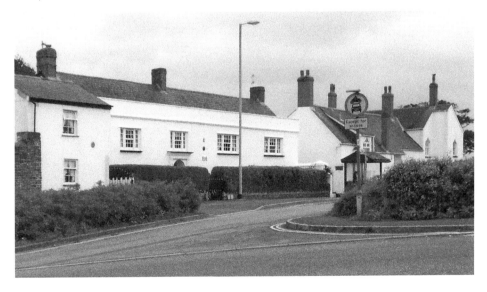

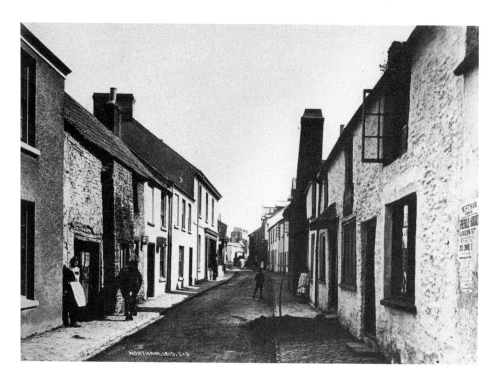

Cross Street

A horse waits patiently outside the forge and there was another blacksmith further along the street. Next door to this one was a butcher's shop and slaughterhouse at the back, which is still there. Northam traders in 1830 included tallow chandlers, mercers, black and whitesmiths, hat manufacturers, lime burners, glass benders, woolstaplers, fellmongers and tawers. No. 58 Cross Street was the site of the village pound, where stray animals were rounded up and impounded to await collection by their owners after payment of a fine. No. 50 Cross Street was an evacuee hostel in the war for children who had special needs and couldn't easily be billeted with host families. Later, it was one of several radio shops.

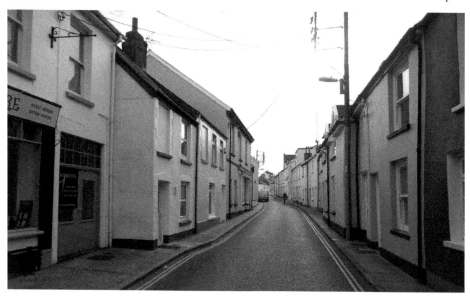

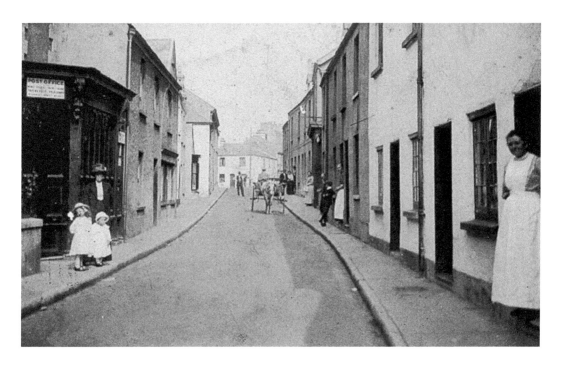

Cross Street

Cross Street and Windmill Lane were once one continuous street leading down to an ancient ford down on the river bank before Bideford Bridge was built, and to the lime kiln and shipbuilders' yards there at Boat Hyde and below Burrough. Later, Cross Street became the main road to Appledore and was subsequently known as Appledore Street, replacing the earlier one down New Causeway Hill. The one-storey building on the left was the post office at this time, replacing an earlier one a little further along the road which then became the Northam Telephone Exchange. Mail was sorted in a side room of the post office, which later moved to Northam Square.

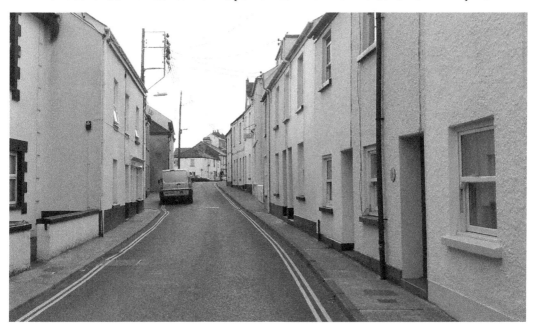

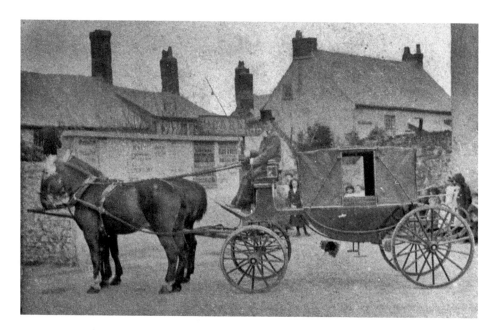

Honey Street

Mr Hearn ran his carriages here at the top of Honey Street at the junction with Cross Street. He was one of several carriers in Northam and Mr Fursdon's stage wagon went to Torrington, Hatherleigh, Tavistock, Plymouth and Hartland. However, in 1855 the railway reached Bideford and the great era of coaching began to draw to a close. By 1902 Mr Hearn was advertising his services as boot and shoe dealer, town crier, bill poster, sexton and then as keeper for Northam of the animal pound here in Cross Street. At the bottom of Honey Street with its junction with North Street was the first Wesleyan chapel. When the new chapel was built in Cross Street, the old chapel became the blacksmith's shop, then later an engineering workshop, eventually being converted to a house. Honey Street was the old road to Appledore leading into Oxman's Lane and then Diddywell Road before New Causeway Hill was built from Northam Square and there was a posting inn in Honey Street.

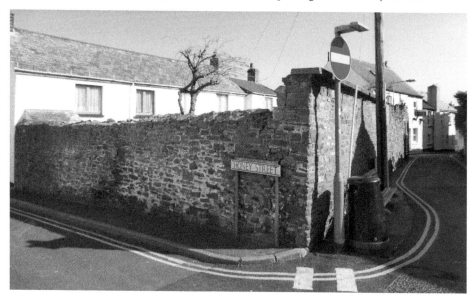

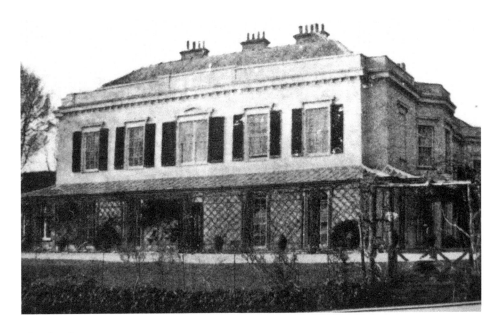

Clevelands

Clevelands was one of the biggest mansions in Northam, now sadly demolished with flats built on the site, though the stables and several drives remain. Lady Mary Bisshopp owned Clevelands in the nineteenth century and left it in her will dated 1891. The next owner was Mr C. S. Carnegie, JP. In February 1906, Bideford Library and Museum was opened by C. S. Carnegie; he was a relative of the great benefactor and philanthropist Andrew Carnegie, whose generosity had enabled the library to be built in the first place and who provided the funding. Before this time, the library had been in a house in Bridgeland Street and then in Bridge Buildings.

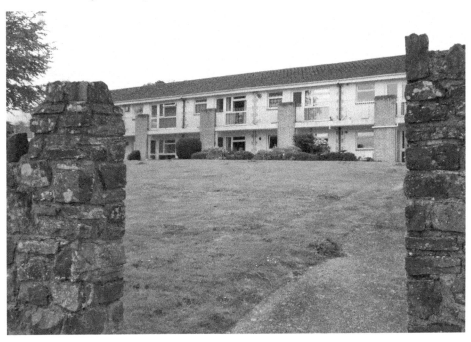

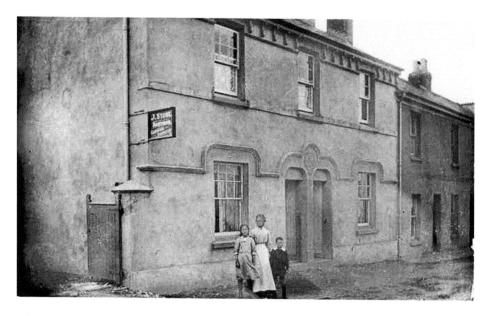

Old Dairy Burrough Road

There were once two farms on the junction of Burrough Road and Cross Street. The building in the picture was once Withecombe's Farm and it had a granary at the back. Cows were brought into the yard at times and a dairy behind the farmhouse involved the cows being herded along the village roads. There was also a farm opposite, which belonged to the Pennington family, who also brought their cows into the yard behind for milking. There was another farm in Cross Street by the Swan Inn. Many villages had farmhouses within the curtilage of the village; the cows were taken to outlying fields by day and brought back to the village farmhouse for milking and for milk distribution.

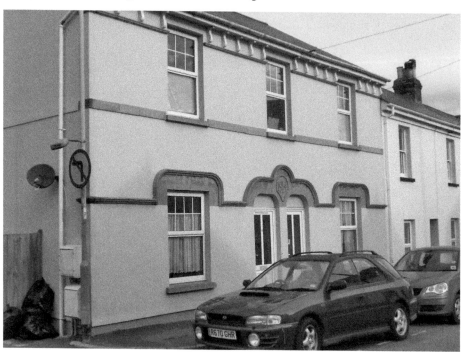

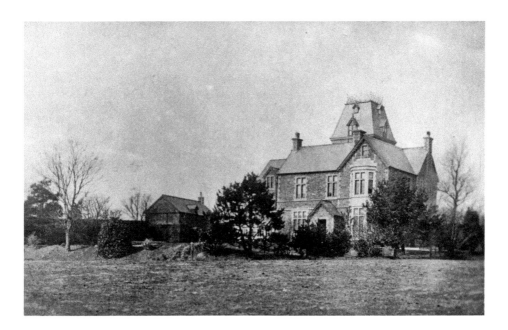

Conybeare Bay View Road

Bay View Road was originally known as Sanctuary Lane as it led to a chantry chapel at the entrance to the Tors, known as Chapel Field, by the house called Tors Top. Like many Northam mansions, Conybear was occupied by a retired officer. John Babbington and his wife Mary had eight children and two live-in servants. During the war, the tower was used by the local Home Guard and firewatchers kept watch every night to look out for bombs, enemy attacks and fires. An auction sale in 1888 advertised it as having 'lawn tennis grounds, orchard house, two stall stables, loose boxes, coach house, harness room, lofts, piggery, thirteen bed and dressing rooms, library, butler's pantry, servants' hall, lumber room, cellars and an ample water supply with a well and pump.'

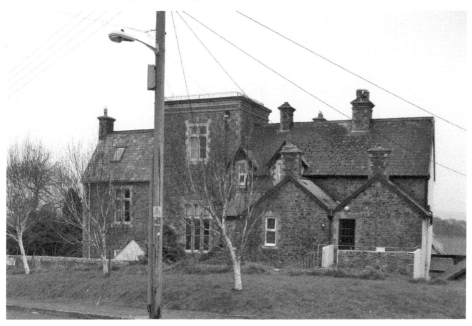

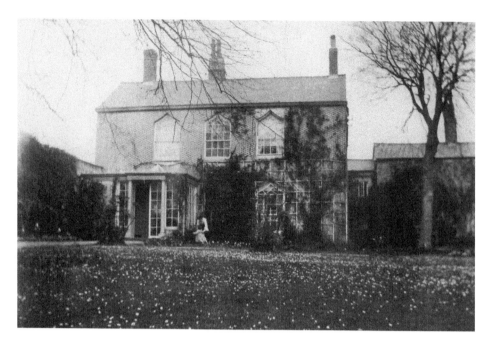

Northam House

Northam House was probably built in 1654 during the reign of Charles II when he was King of Scotland and Ireland and Oliver Cromwell had declared himself Lord Protector of England. It was a large house with extensive grounds, but the new road to Appledore was driven through here and cut through a large part of the garden and the tennis court. The stables and coach house at the side were converted into cottages and the Foxhill estate was built in the orchard and further gardens. The right-hand wing set back was the servants' wing and the furthest right-hand house was the accommodation for the housekeeper and gardeners. Judge Jeffries is reputed to have stayed at the house at one time and he executed a man outside one of the bedroom windows where the war memorial now stands.

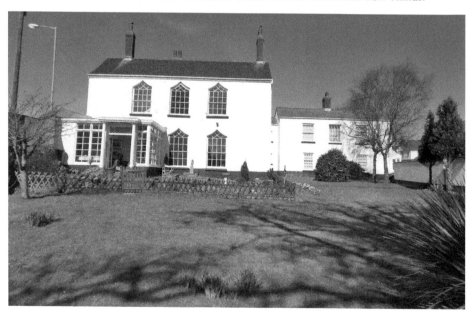

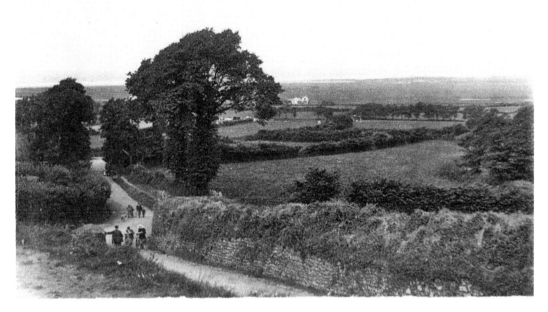

Sandymere Road, Looking North from Bone Hill

Originally known as Pimpley Road, this road led down to Northam station and on over the level crossing down to the Burrows from Northam village. No houses have been built in the area of the photograph yet. At the bottom of the road was Pimpley Farm, later renamed North House. Water was pumped up from wells at Pimpley to fill the new reservoirs, which had been built above Westward Ho! to supply their water. The golf club is in the distance. There was an RAF radar station at the lower end of Pimpley Road, with pylons bordering the Burrows. There were concrete bomb shelters and large Nissen huts to house service personnel stationed there. After the war, the UK faced a massive shortage of housing and civilians lived in these Nissen huts for a time, though the cold interior walls ran with condensation in the winter.

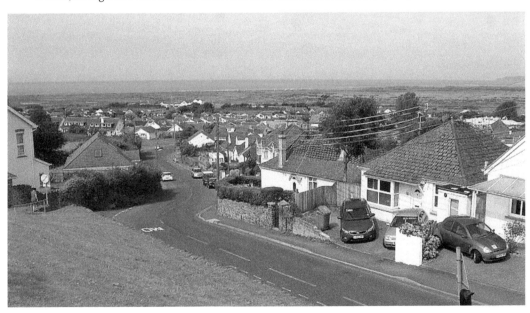

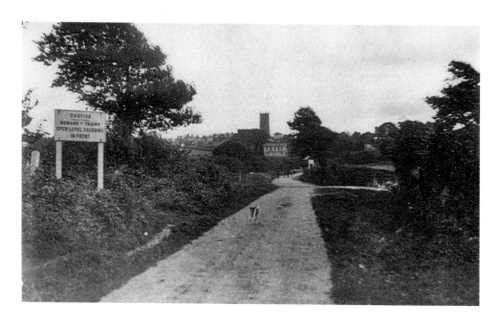

Sandymere/Pimpley Road Looking South, *c.* 1910

We are almost at the site of Northam station with the level crossing of the BWH&A Railway crossing the road here, just beyond the notice that reads 'Caution. Beware of Trains. Open Level Crossing in Front.' Northam church tower is on the skyline and Golf Links Road is coming in from the right just before the railway track. Northam station was opened in 1901 and closed in 1917. It opened as the terminus of the railway for a while and the track ran to a buffer stop with a runaround loop for the engine, a siding and a signal box, though all of these were removed when the line was extended to Appledore and the station was demoted to being called a halt. It had a small waiting room and lavatory on the platform. Until 1990 there were some old steps remaining here, and the track of the line continuing on towards Appledore is still a footpath for a short length.

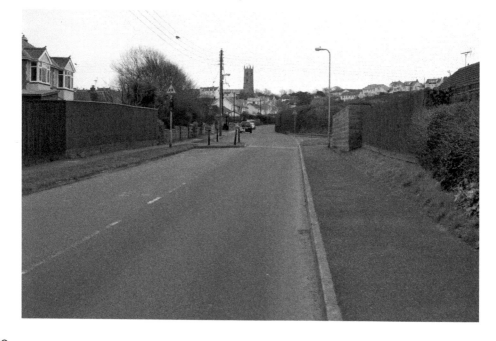

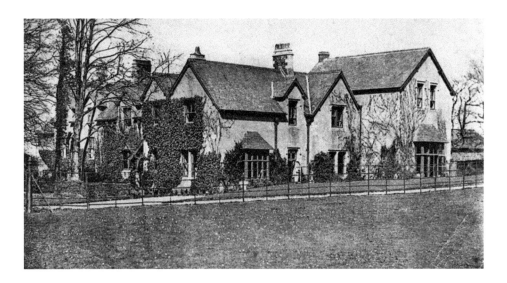

Burrough House

There has been an ancient manor house here for at least 500 years and it still bears the name of the Burrough Family who owned it then. It was the home of Steven and William Borough. Steven Borough was born here in 1525 and he named the North Cape in 1553, and was one of the masters to have the keeping and oversight of the Navy under Queen Elizabeth I. His younger brother, William, was born in 1536 and was Commander of the Golden Lion, Comptroller of the Queen's Navy and was a vice admiral under Sir Francis Drake in 1590. They are commemorated in the name Burrough Road and the Golden Lion pub in Cross Street. But it was not to these two illustrious sons that their father, John Borough, left the estate. When John died in 1570 at the age of seventy-six, he made his daughter Agnes his heir instead, and she and her husband Thomas Leigh succeeded to the ownership of Burrough House. They became very wealthy and rebuilt the house in 1589, which was then much admired for its elegant design, and they bought up the manor of Northam to go with the house. By 1779, the house was called Burrow in the Land Tax records and was much mourned when Captain William Yeo demolished the graceful old mansion and built two much plainer semi-detached houses in its place.

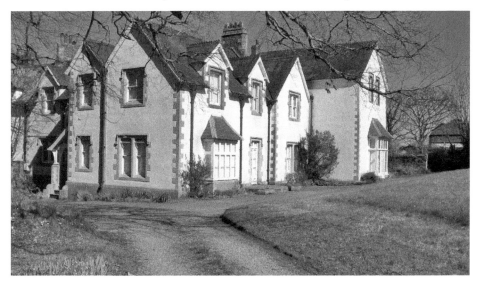

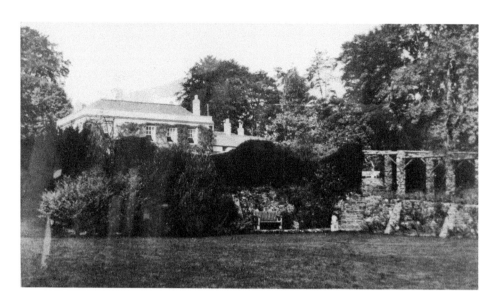

Durrant House, Durrant Lane

So many of Northam's great mansions have been demolished and are gone forever. Durrant House is another that appears to have disappeared but is still there underneath if you know where to look. Here is a photograph of Durrant House Hotel viewed from the gardens at the back of the hotel; the original mansion can still be seen on the right of the picture rather enveloped in more modern additions and with a third storey added as well. A very old house stood here in the eighteenth century known as Derrent in 1770, but by 1810 this house had been bought by Sir Richard Keats, son of the Rector of Bideford, and a commander in the Navy when Bideford was the third-largest port in the UK. He eventually became Lord High Admiral of the Fleet and served with Lord Nelson in the West Indies and at the Battle of Trafalgar. He retired to live at his house, Durrant. Durrant House became a successful hotel in about 1973 and has been extended several times.

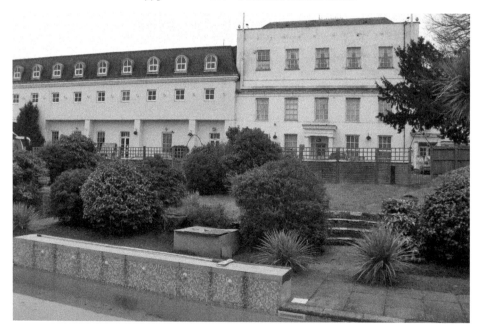

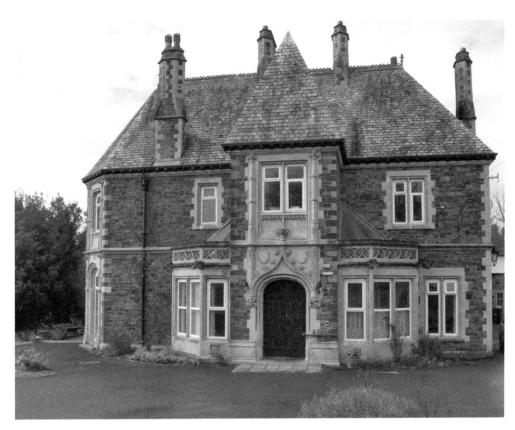

Orphans at Fairlea Children's Home, Chope Road, c. 1945

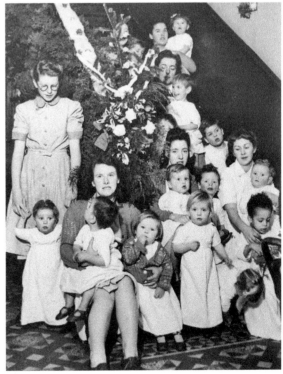

Fairlea was built in around 1872 in a grand Victorian country house style. It was typical of the extravagant, impressive houses built at this time, with its medieval-style front porch, carved columns and Minton floor tiles. It has huge stained-glass windows and a high, grand staircase with its roof open to the rafters and hammer beamed roof suggestive of a church. The cellar was constructed with Romanesque vaulting like a church crypt. By the 1930s, Fairlea had become an orphanage, and remained so till it was commandeered in Second World War by the American Army for billeting their officers. After the war, Fairlea reverted to being a children's home again until it finally closed in 1954. For two years it remained empty and unused and then it reopened as a retirement home. It has been extended hugely at the back of the old house.

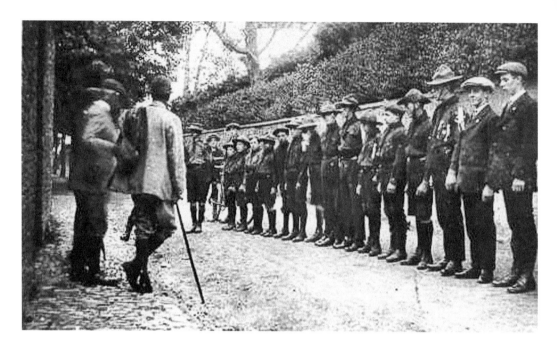

Bay View Road, *c.* 1912

The 2nd Northam Scouts are lining up here outside the present Northam Health Centre and the pavement is cobbled and the road just dried earth. The old barn behind the Scout leaders was probably once part of Muddix Farm and is still there. At that time it was the Scout Hut, later becoming the Northam Library, and now it is the pharmacy attached to the Health Centre. Like so many other buildings in the area, it was even requisitioned in the Second World War and taken over as a casualty wound dressing station and for blood donors to help the wounded. The hedges and trees behind the scouts are in the gardens of Hanover House, a big mansion with large gardens whose drive came out into Bay View Road here. Bay View Court has now been built on its site.

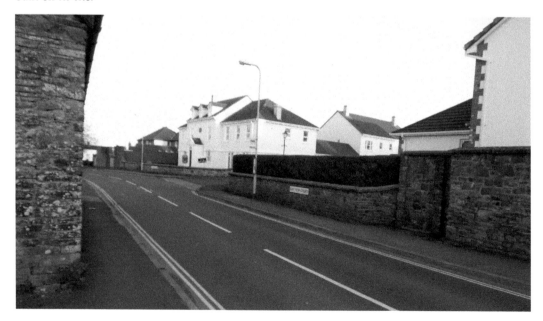

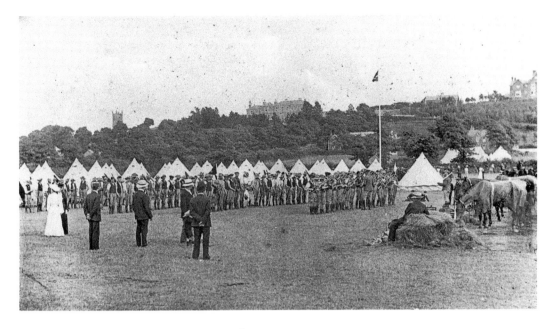

Commons Farm Yeomanry Camp, July 1905

The Northam, Westward Ho! & Appledore Railway transported the Yeomanry every summer to their camp at Commons Farm, Westward Ho! The occasion became a sort of fête for the local people and sightseers, with Northam and Westward Ho! decorated with flags and bunting. On the skyline, left to right, is Northam church tower, then Lakenham House, then the lodge and stables to the big house called Commons (later Belmont, which was demolished and Dolphin Court built in its place). Commons had its main drive from Piggy Lane, now just a green lane. Lakenham was built for the Duchess of Manchester.

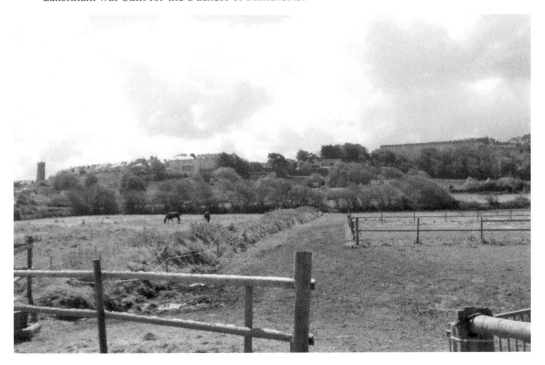

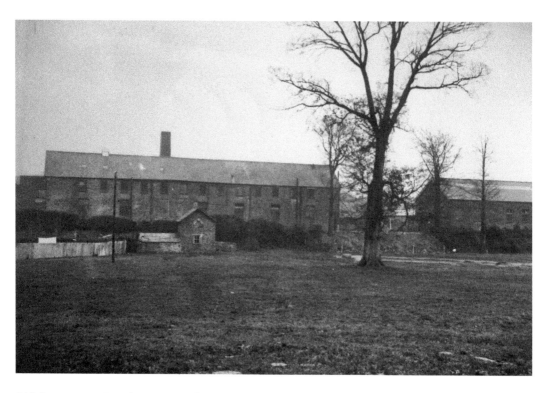

Old Cement Works, Chanters Road

Chanters Road was once called Chanters Lane and it snaked along to the riverbank here where there were old shipyards and these cementworks just where Torridge District Council Riverside offices now stand. The fields in front were once the site of the main Bideford cattle market but they have now been replaced by a car park.

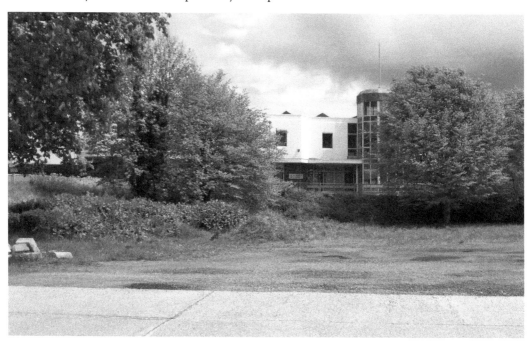

Northam Windmills

There were once two windmills near the centre of Northam. The foundations and a millstone were found in the gardens of No. 24 Windmill Lane in the 1960s, where one of the windmills was sited, though there is no longer any trace of the windmill itself. Thomas Leigh of Burrough House owned it once. It was called 'Lane' and he left it in his will to his wife in 1609 together with his house 'Borowe'. The second windmill was called Bidna Mill and was let in 1806 and advertised as having 'a brisk wind which would grind twelve bushels of corn in an hour'. It was then rented by George Causey who lived at Knapp Farm. Only remnants of this mill remain in the field at Bidna but many of the bricks can still be seen on the beach at Watertown near the old Hinks' Boatyard. They were cemented together in an attempt to strengthen the sea wall there.

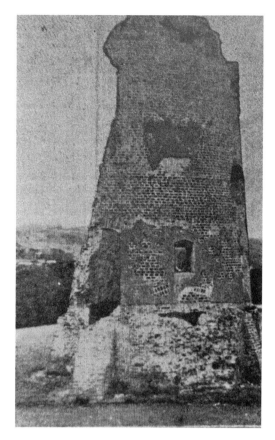

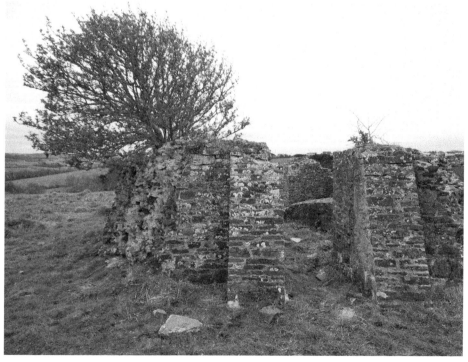

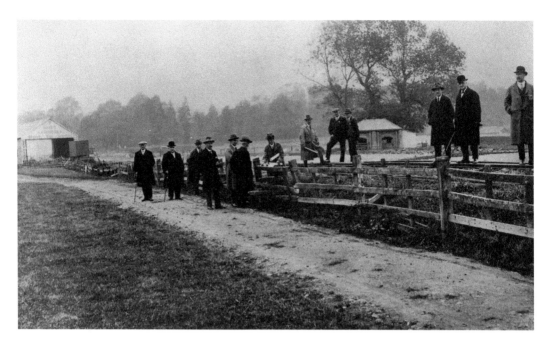

Making of the Kingsley Road, 1924, the New Road to Northam
For 500 years, Northam Causeway was the main road from Bideford to Northam, which was laid across the marsh. However, when the railway closed, the track of the line was converted to be a new road – the present Kingsley Road. In both the new and old photographs we are standing on the present Bideford football ground and looking across at the Kingsley Road being constructed. The old engine shed on the left of the photograph was one of two railway sheds. In the old picture, Hardy Colwills have taken it over for their new motor buses and the notice reads, 'Motor bus services.' In the new picture it is Heard's Coaches. The football ground was Curtis' Marsh and was a very waterlogged area occasionally used by travelling circuses.

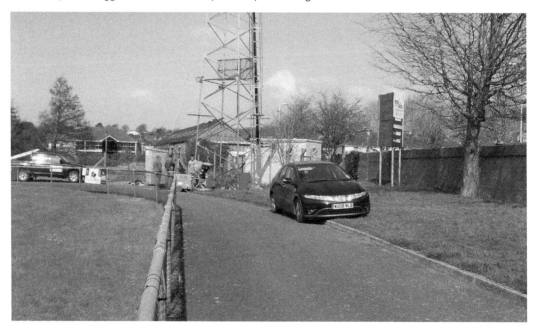

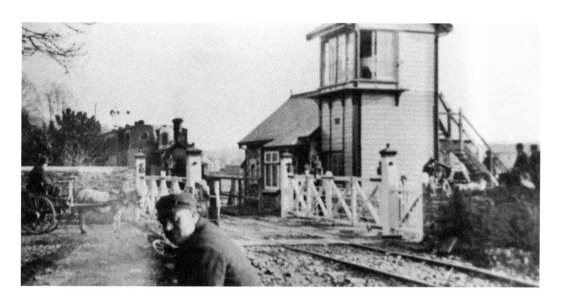

Causeway Crossing Northam Road

This was one of the numerous halts on the line of the BWH&A Railway. This causeway was once the main road to Northam from Bideford before 1925. We are standing on the actual railway line looking towards the level crossing, where a horse and cart wait to cross from the left, another waiting from the right. The train has stopped at the halt beyond the level crossing and there is a signal behind the train. Wooden steps lead up to the two-storey signal box. The crossing keeper's cottage is still there today, though now derelict.

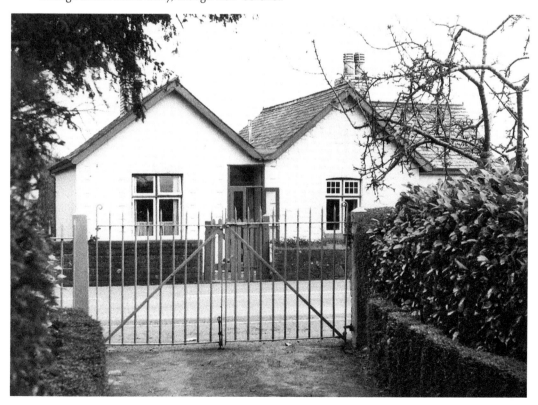

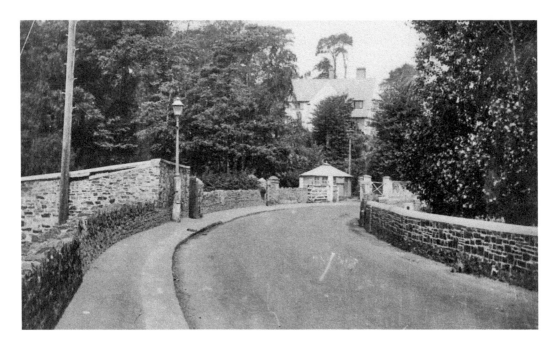

Northam Causeway Crossing

We are looking along the old causeway back towards Bideford and the level crossing of the Westward Ho! Railway. The crossing gate keeper came back from fighting in the First World War to find the railway closed and his job gone. He had always mended people's shoes as a sideline in his signal box, so he set up this ex-Army hut seen on the left of the road, the foundations and wall of which are still there. There he carried on his shoemaking and repair business. His house next to Marsh Farm, called The Causeway, remains in ruins. Later, it was extended over the line of the railway on the Northam side. The drive of the house opposite, called Meadoway, is laid upon the old track bed. The railway track went up the Kenwith Valley through the garden of this house and on through the wood.

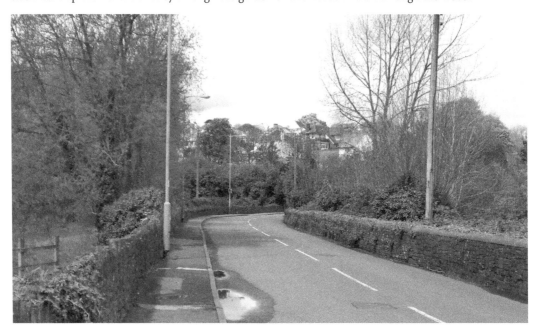

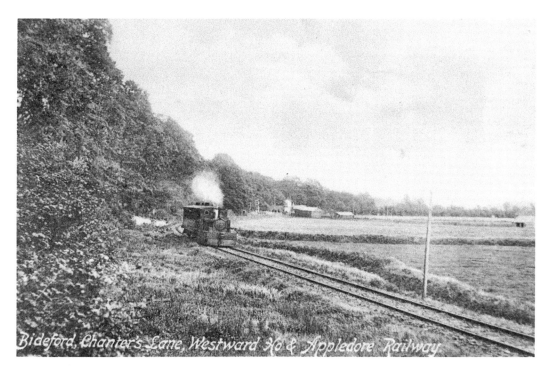

Bideford, Chanter's Lane, Westward Ho & Appledore Railway.

Kenwith Valley Railway Line

A train has just left the Causeway Crossing Halt and is steaming up the Kenwith Valley to its next stop at Kenwith Castle Halt. Causeway signal box is in the background and also a signal post. The train here is near the site of Kenwith Valley flood protection lakes.

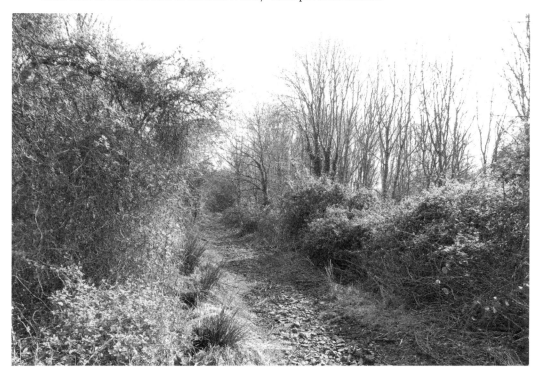

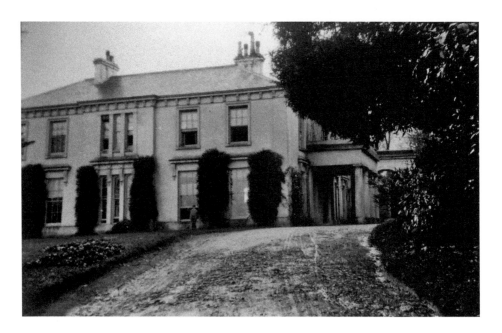

Hallsannery

It comes as a surprise to many people to realise that Northam continues on the far Torrington side of Bideford and is known as Northam Without or Northam Ridge. Like Northam itself, it was owned by Queen Matilda, wife of the Duke of Normandy, who gave Northam to St Stephen's church in Caen when she was dying, together with its other part Aisserugia (or Ashridge); it is still part of the same ancient manor. Hallsannery is part of this disconnected section of Northam Without, together with a farm still called Ashridge, Bull Head Farm and White Hall, and some very large old lime kilns called Hallsannery Kilns. In 1851, the owner of White Hall was described as a lime merchant and maltster, and was probably working these lime kilns at this time. The lime kilns are still there on the floodplain of the Torridge down by the river and Northam Without had its own brickyard.

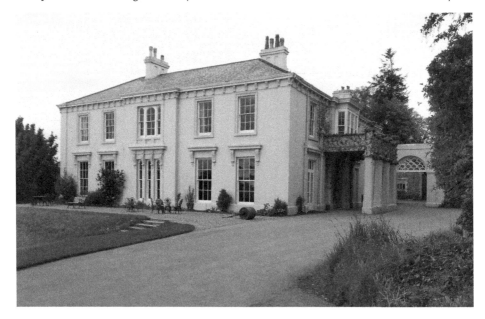

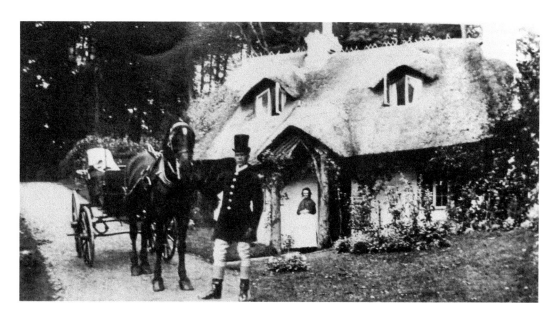

Lodge to Moreton House, Jennetts Cottage, Buckland Road

Moreton House, originally called Daddon, was the home of the Stucleys who were the fifth biggest landowner in the whole of Devon, once with 19,800 acres! There were various drives with lodges to the house going to the Abbotsham and Clovelly roads and this one was added later on going down to the new Bradworthy turnpike road. This lodge, a cottage, still exists on the old Buckland Brewer road by the side of the carriage drive bridge going over the road shown to the left of the lodge and now a grassy track.

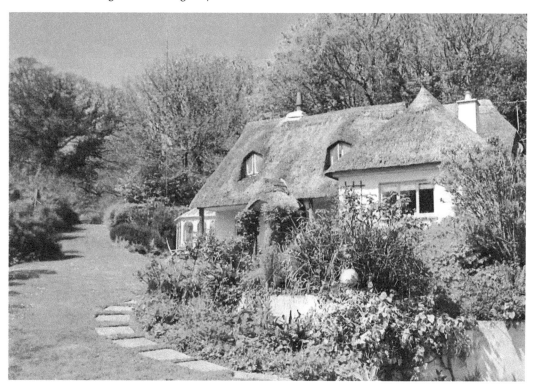

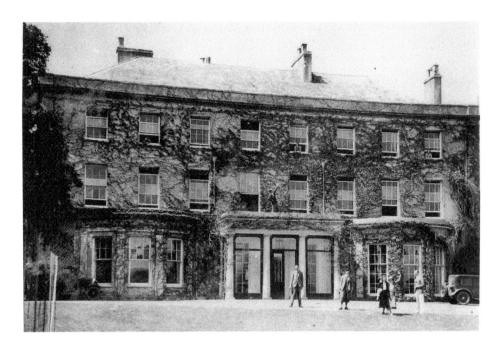

Moreton House/Daddon House

This was once the house and lands of the Grenville family who were lords of the manor of Bideford. British naval commander Sir Richard Grenville (1541–91) of *The Revenge* was the person whose family in later years owned the Moreton estate, or Daddon as it was originally called. *The Revenge* was Francis Drake's flagship in the battle against the Spanish Armada. By the eighteenth century, George Stucley Buck owned the estate. In 1760, George Buck started rebuilding the old Daddon House shortly after his marriage to Anne Orchard, heiress of Hartland Abbey. His son changed the name to Moreton and he and his wife improved the park and added drives and lodges.

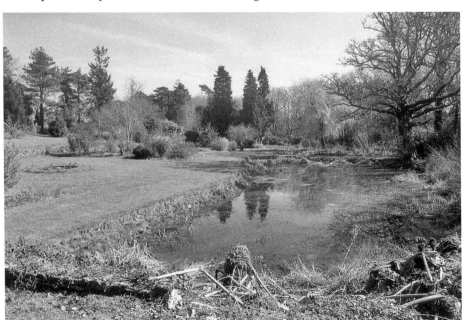

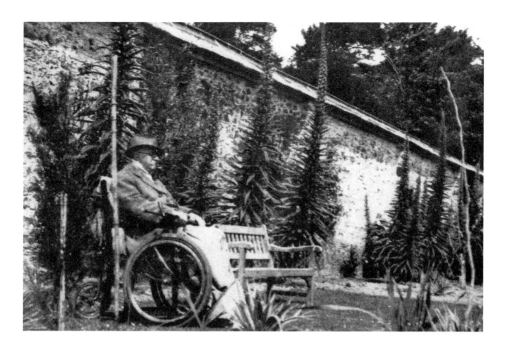

Moreton House Gardens

In 1913 Sir Hugh Grenville Stucley and his wife inherited the Moreton estate, and being keen gardeners created beautiful parterres, terraces, a pergola, a summerhouse, a subtropical walled garden and a water garden with a series of lakes and waterfalls. His son, Sir Dennis, lived at Hartland Abbey and decided to sell Moreton, which became part of Grenville College School. Moreton was sold off when Grenville College merged with Edgehill College. Despite valiant efforts to save them, the future of the magnificent gardens hangs in the balance, but what a wonderful public park this could be for Bideford.

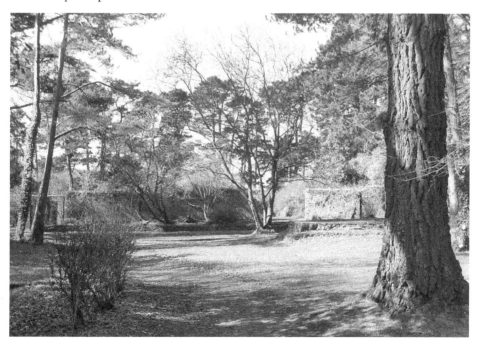

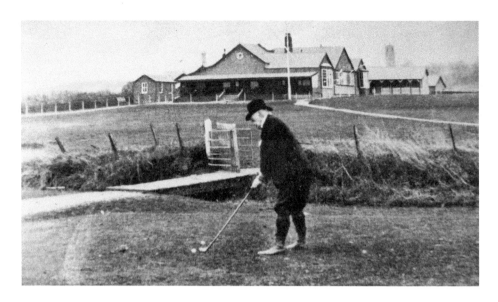

Royal North Devon Golf Club

Founded in 1864, the RND is the oldest golf course in England. Golf was a new game then and described as 'something like croquet' or as 'that damned Scottish cricket'! The very first clubhouse was merely a room in the local farmhouse, and then just a bathing machine dragged up from the beach to the first tee. This was superseded by a bell tent, which was dragged out in a handcart from the farmhouse, until at last an iron hut was built right up against the pebble ridge (described as looking like a dog kennel). After playing, Molesworth would gallop to the Pebbleridge Hotel along the pebble ridge. The iron hut was only big enough for a table, a few benches and a rough bar counter, but players stored their clubs here and it served them for a while, until a big storm sent waves crashing over it. It was time to move and it was taken further inland near the Inland Sea. Its foundations are still there.

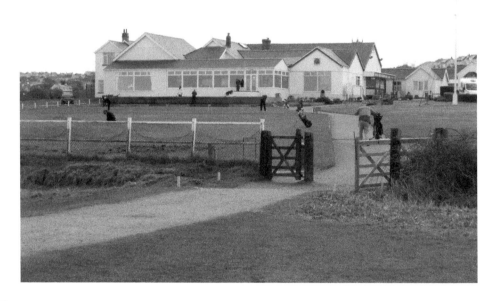

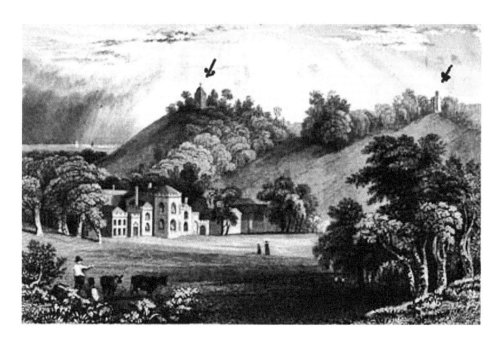

Kenwith Castle

Kenwith Castle, the Grade II listed mansion, was built around 1760 in Georgian Castellated Gothic style and originally called Kenwith Lodge. Crenellated walls flank the sides of the building, and there are interesting pointed arches over the windows and particularly beautiful decorations inside with panelling and carved mouldings. It has been extended several times and is now a retirement home. Two ornate, pretty little Georgian summer houses were built on slopes behind the castle and are shown prominently in the etching. One still exists in a neighbouring garden. Kenwith Castle was named after the ancient earthwork in the grounds of the house and associated with a Viking battle in local folklore. When the Westward Ho! Railway was built, Kenwith Castle got its own private railway station to serve the house. Called Kenwith Castle Halt, it was only ever a request halt for the owners. There was an ungated level crossing on the drive to the castle and a small wooden platform, but no shelter was provided for the sparse number of passengers.

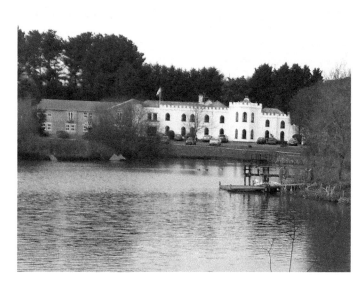

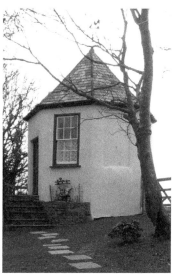

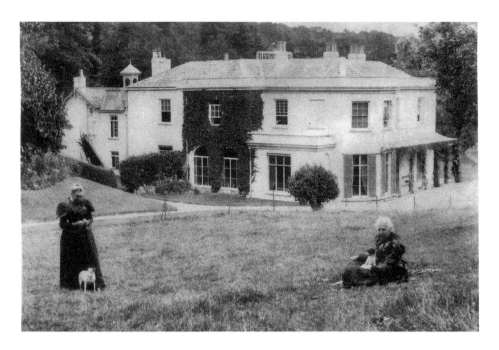

Lenwood

An ancient site first referred to in 1330 as Lyndwode (lime tree wood) and then known as Lendwood in the 1770s, this was the home of the Wren family in the nineteenth century, including extensive land holdings. The armed forces took over the house during the war and built sheds and Nissen huts. By 1945, the house had been bought by the enterprising Dampier-Bennetts, who first tried farming there and then began manufacturing potato crisps in the farm sheds. The next enterprise was to convert the grounds, house and sheds into a holiday camp in the late 1950s, and they built a swimming pool for the guests and chalets in the gardens. Sold in 1969, the house became a restaurant, sports club and country club with tennis courts and heated swimming pool, all much used by local people. Permission was granted for holiday houses to be built in the grounds and they were eventually permitted to be permanent housing.

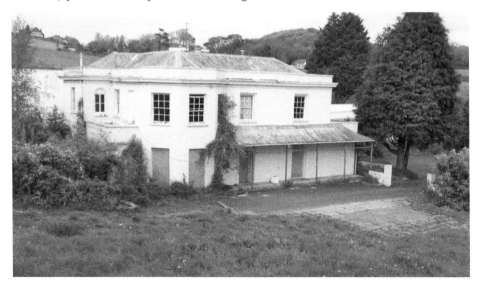

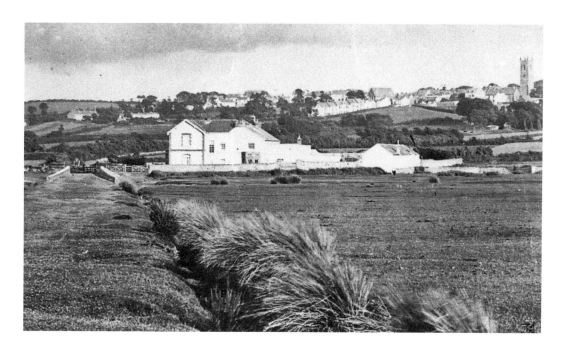

North House, Sandymere Road

North House was also known as Pimpley House when Sandymere Road was called Pimpley Road. The house was on a very ancient site and was one of the few farmhouses on the old grazing lands of Northam Burrows. It was called Pempillys in 1857 when William Pickard was farming here on this poor, unproductive land. There were wells here from which water was pumped up to the storage reservoirs high above the new Westward Ho! to supply the villas and hotels there. The house was requisitioned during the war and because of its proximity to RAF Northam and the radar station near the house, RAF officers were billeted here. The farmhouse was demolished and three bungalows built on the site.

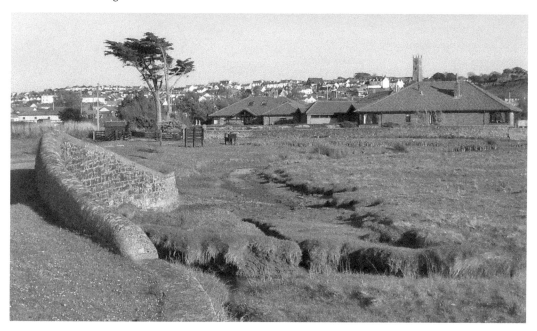

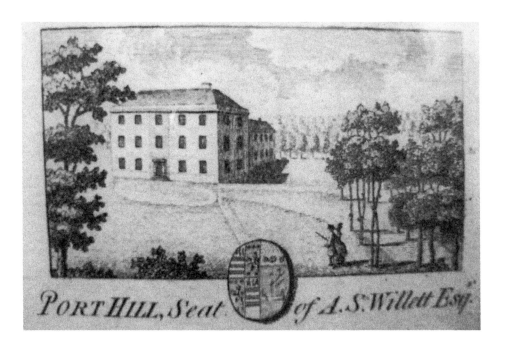

PORT HILL, Seat ... of A. S. Willett Esq

Port Hill in 1790 and 2010

Porthill was built around 1760 by the Willetts family. Originally, the house was much taller and had three storeys so that the owners could see the estuary and watch ships entering the port of Bideford as seen in the old 1790 picture. However, they found that the house was too exposed to the wind and decided to remove the top storey. The estate was large and extensive and included all the land that would later become Clevelands to the north, running right down to the land beyond Chanters Lane and the border with Bideford. Later, the house was let to Admiral Sir Richard Keats in 1820 and he had great fun signalling from his hilltop retreat at Port Hill to his friend at Cross House, Torrington (Stevens Guile). The house was auctioned in 1884 and advertised as having 35 acres, stables and orchard houses; Admiral Charlewood lived there then. Later still, the house became a girls' school, which eventually closed in 1889 and the kitchen garden became a market garden for a time. The present drive onto Heywood Road still has old stables at the bottom, but an old cottage there was demolished when Heywood Road was widened. Other drives went across in the other direction to Lenwood Road and another ran down the hill to rejoin Heywood Road further down.

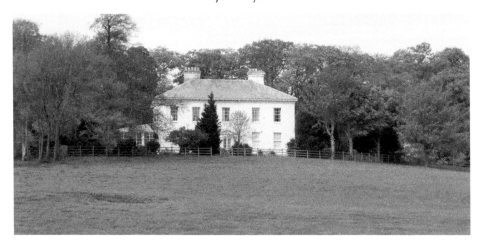

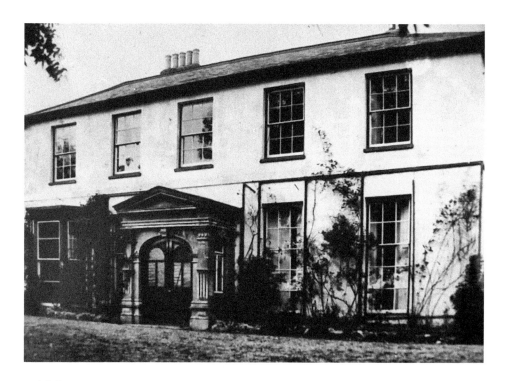

Raleigh House

Raleigh has always been associated with the well-known Devon family of Sir Walter Raleigh, and legend has it that the family did have a house here on this hill and that he landed his first shipment of tobacco in the port of Bideford. It is an ancient site referred to in the Lay Subsidy Rolls of 1333 as Rylegh and then as Ryley in 1695, probably meaning a rye field. By 1779 it was Raileigh, then called Rawleigh House by 1856 when the Cockshott family were living here. By that time it was a huge estate. Raleigh has now been divided up into multiple residences but at least it lives on!

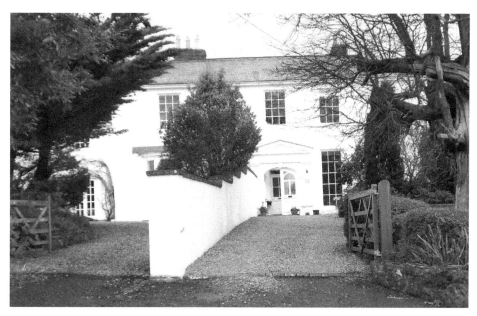

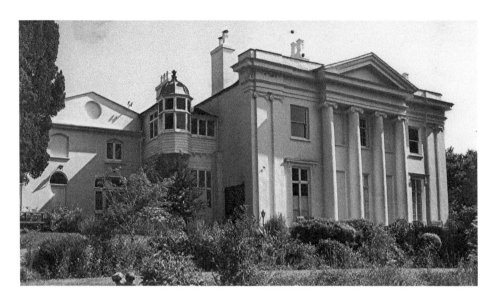

Woodville, Northam's Hidden Mansion

Northam's most beautiful Palladian mansion with its Ionic pilasters and pedimented gable came within an ace of being completely lost to dereliction and demolition. It was built in around 1820 for £500 for an officer in the British Indian Army, though strangely the stable block, now part of the house, is even older. By 1937 the Haime family was living there and the three daughters who inherited the house lived on in the crumbling mansion within the wilderness of the garden in just one room, almost as recluses, and eventually died there. Efforts to sell the house were unsuccessful in the recession of 1991 and Woodville entered its darkest period. The house and grounds were left empty and abandoned, thieves smashed the windows and broke in and stole the marble fireplaces, the beautiful circular mahogany staircase and the panelled mahogany doors and ransacked the house. It was boarded up and the magnificent gardens became completely overgrown with thick brambles and trees. In spite of being Grade II listed, the house was almost lost until at last a buyer, Doug Whitehead, stepped in to rescue it and turn it into an early digital media centre, with twenty employees working in its magnificent rooms. The photograph shows the south front of the house facing the lake, along with the stable block on the left, which has now been incorporated into the house.

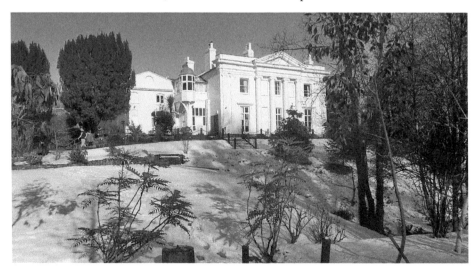

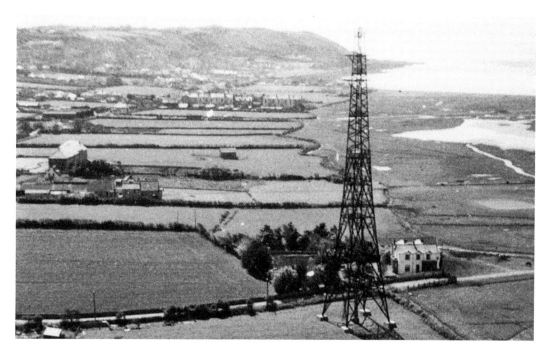

Northam and Westward Ho!'s Secret War

Westward Ho! was heavily involved in the Second World War, with many of its mansions and large houses requisitioned for Army personnel and for housing evacuated schools. Out on Northam Burrows the ground was heavily mined to keep out the enemy and inquisitive locals, and top-secret military operations were being carried out. At the bottom of the slipway, the beach was fenced off heavily with barbed wire and a gun emplacement and the pebble ridge was mined. In 1941, the RAF established a radar station on the Burrows known as RAF Northam. It was a Chain Home radar station, capable of detecting high-flying aircraft at long ranges and set up on the Burrows and adjacent fields. The station had two pairs of steel transmitter masts, 325 feet high, with a curtain array slung between them; two timber receiver towers 240 feet high and two transmitter blocks in which radar personnel worked; a generator house; Nissen huts; air-raid shelters; a guard post and defence positions. RAF officers were billeted at North House. The station closed in 1944 because there was a severe housing shortage after the war and civilians lived in the Nissen huts. The receiver block remains on the Follyfoot Equestrian Centre and can be seen from the road. Other local radar stations were at RAF Hartland Point and RAF Wrafton. The photograph shows one of the transmitter masts at the bottom of Sandymere Road with North House/Pimpley House just to the right of it.

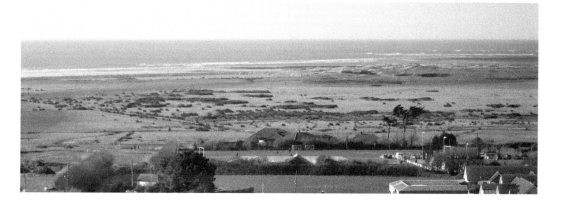

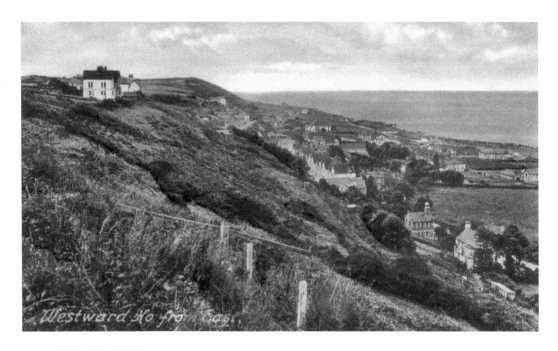

Westward Ho from ...

Lost Old Road at Northam

The upper picture is a rare photograph of the old road, now lost, which once came steeply down from the top of Bay View Road near Edgehill (in the background) to Tadworthy and Northam Burrows. The lower image is of another lost old road down to the Burrows, also from Bay View Road. Called Piggy Lane it begins near Northam Surgery, and is still a bridle path. Seen at the right angle bend is the old entrance and lodge to Commons (later called Belmont), which was accessed from Piggy Lane at this time. Belmont became part of Stella Maris Convent School and was used as a boarding house at one time. Later, Belmont was demolished and Dolphin Court built in its place.

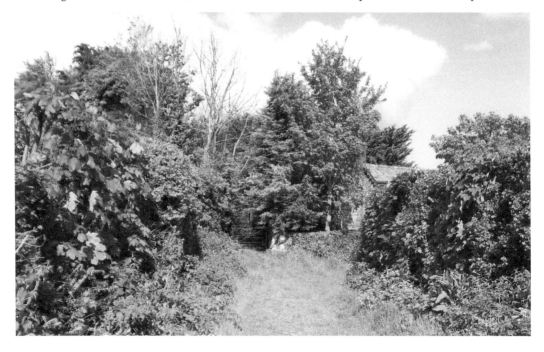

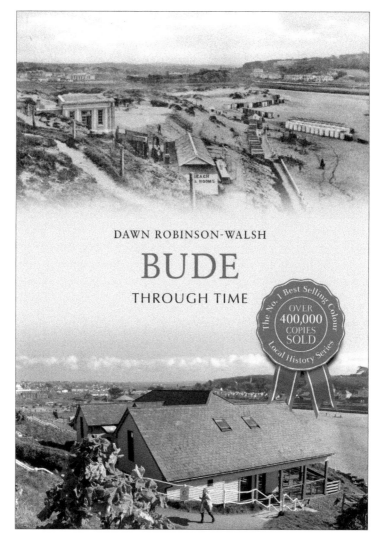

Bude Through Time

Dawn Robinson-Walsh

This fascinating selection of photographs traces some of the many ways in which Bude has changed and developed over the last century.

978 1 4456 1797 8

96 pages, full colour

Available from all good bookshops or order direct
from our website www.amberleybooks.com

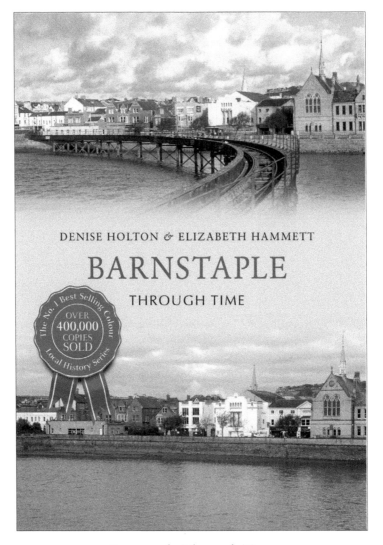

Barnstaple Through Time

Denise Holton & Elizabeth Hammett

This fascinating selection of photographs traces some of the many
ways in which Barnstaple has changed and developed over the last
century.

978 1 4456 0851 8

96 pages, full colour